THE ROMAN STONECUTTER

THE ROMAN STONECUTTER

An Introduction to Latin Epigraphy

GIANCARLO SUSINI

Edited with an introduction by
E. Badian

Translated by A. M. Dabrowski

OXFORD · BASIL BLACKWELL

Printed and bound in Great Britain by The Camelot Press Ltd, London and Southampton

CONTENTS

LIST OF PLATES

Between pages 22 and 23

EDITOR'S INTRODUCTION

The study of inscriptions gives us an opportunity for an immediacy of contact with ancient life, such as no other discipline within the field of ancient studies (except for the special and limited case of papyrology) can provide. Literature provides valuable access to a privileged élite; archaeology can give us something of the feel of daily life by revealing the objects of the physical environment. But the élite was relatively small and not representative of ordinary people, and the objects are mute. It is only the inscription that actually speaks to us as it did to contemporaries. The epigraphist, for this very reason, cannot isolate himself within an autonomous discipline. He must be a historian and an archaeologist, a palaeographer and a philologist, drawing on—and in turn contributing to—all these disciplines and others. In a sense, he stands at the centre of ancient studies.

Unfortunately, epigraphy has not been much taught in the traditional Classics course and in courses on ancient history and life, except for the use of 'documents' as evidence for the historian. Although experience has shown that it makes an immediate appeal to students—even students with only a very elementary knowledge of the ancient languages—and infuses life into a study that they are often encouraged to pursue in an abstract and theoretical way, few of us are trained to teach it, and there are few books that can be used in the sort of courses we ought to be designing.

It is not surprising that the original Italian edition of Professor Susini's little book on Latin inscriptions was sold out and had to be reprinted within two years, and it is a pleasure to have helped to make it available in English. Professor Susini takes us behind the scenes, as it were, enabling us to watch the stone being quarried and carefully prepared, the decoration being applied, the customer coming into the workshop and either setting out his ideas or (more often, perhaps) making his choice, on the advice of the foreman, to suit his needs and his purse. Starting from a clear exposition of recent advances in the palaeographical study of Latin inscriptions—a field to which he has made original contributions—he takes us on a fascinating journey of exploration into the realms of technology, psychology and *Kulturgeschichte*, to which that study, rightly used, provides the key. Many of us, both teachers and students, will be delighted to follow him and, encouraged by his example, to go off exploring on our own, to the extent of our more limited knowledge and experience.

It has been pleasant to renew and improve my acquaintance with this book, in the firm hope that it will now brighten many a classroom in English-speaking countries. The translator's knowledge of Italian and of Classics provided a firm foundation, and Professor Susini was (expectedly) co-operative both on details of interpretation and on the few questions that arose in adapting the book to a public not familiar with Italy. In fact, changes have been kept to a minimum, since the author's ideas and his choice of examples form an integral whole. Although a work of this kind written by an author with an English or American background would obviously be different, it is perhaps a further charm of this book that it took shape against a background that most of us treasure.

I should like to record a special debt of gratitude to Professor and Mrs. A. E. Gordon, who were generous with advice and help at all stages of production. But for their patience and accuracy, there would have been many more errors than (through no fault of theirs) will inevitably remain. I should also like to thank my former colleague, Mr. R. P. Wright, for advice on some points of detail.

Harvard University   E. BADIAN
December 1972

ABBREVIATIONS

Journals have been abbreviated according to the standard listing in *L'Année philologique*, where this was available. Where it was not, titles have either been given in full or printed with minimal abbreviation. For the various collections of inscriptions, the standard abbreviations by initials have been used:

CIL= *Corpus Inscriptionum Latinarum*
IG= *Inscriptiones Graecae*
ILLRP= A. Degrassi (ed.), *Inscriptiones Latinae Liberae Rei Publicae*
ILS= H. Dessau (ed.), *Inscriptiones Latinae Selectae*
Note *Inscr. It.*= *Inscriptiones Italiae*

AUTHOR'S NOTE

The examples of inscriptions cited are intended merely as illustrations. Many others could have been put on record, to confirm and amplify both reports of observation and statements of fact. Every inscription referred to has been seen by the author and all discussion is based on the original stones.

I

EPIGRAPHY AND
PALAEOGRAPHY

There is no doubt that the study of Roman epigraphy has been greatly advanced—or at least, has been moved in a new direction—by the work that Jean Mallon and the other scholars who follow his lead have done in the field of palaeography. Yet though Mallon has made a great contribution to epigraphic studies, I believe, as I shall try to explain in the following pages, that in so doing he has lost sight of, or at least has neglected, the real purpose of epigraphy, which is not to study the history of writing in general, even though epigraphy contributes substantially to this field of study. Having said this, I have no hesitation in concurring with Mallon when he states (almost in deliberate opposition to Mommsen, who saw the nineteenth century as the century of inscriptions) that the twentieth century is the century of *inscriptions and papyri*, appraised, as far as the palaeographer is concerned, from the same point of view and by the same methods.[1] This enthusiasm of Mallon is well known to all who have read his 'Pierres fautives'[2] and who, remembering the numberless analogous instances they have met in their own experience as epigraphists, have felt the impulse to ascertain whether, by the radical application of the methods suggested by Mallon, a satisfactory explanation might be found for a strange name, an unusual word form, a senseless tangle of letters, and not least for the notorious 'stonecutter's error'.

Jean Mallon has expressed his views in a series of articles of extraordinary interest,[3] published after his *Paléographie romaine* (1952).[4] In this earlier work he had already drawn attention to some critical aspects of the study of epigraphy, such as, for instance, the vagueness of the term 'inscription', a term that is now applied to any document written on durable or semi-durable material and thus excludes anything written on papyrus or on parchment. (Although I should point out that Etruscologists do not hesitate to classify the writing on the bands of the Zagreb mummy among 'epigraphic' documents.) Mallon, in short, sees things from the palaeographer's point of view; accordingly, and quite appropriately, he warns against applying different methods to writing on stone and to writing on papyrus: in other words, against subordinating the graphic interpretation of a *texte* to the *pièce* on which it is written. Already in his *Paléographie*, speaking of a well-known shop sign from Palermo (with which we shall deal later), Mallon had observed that, within the same shop, the work had to pass through different stages before the engraving could be done. In his subsequent papers—summing up numerous observations made by scholars (particularly Hübner[5] and Cagnat[6]) on epigraphic texts and ancient sources over the last seventy years —he has definitively distinguished the different stages of work in the mason's shop, or what we might more appropriately call the different phases in the genesis of an epigraphic document. There are three of these stages: first, the drafting of the text; next, the transfer of the text on to the stone in the shape of a provisional outline, the *ordinatio*, meant to guide the hand of the stonecutter; lastly, the actual carving. Of these three stages, the first is undeniably the most important from the point of view of the history of writing, and therefore the most important for the proper exegesis of the document. Unfortunately, however, this is also the stage which, as far as we know, has left no trace. The copy of the draft for an epigraphic text, drawn up each time—according to Mallon—on perishable writing material, was thrown away after use, and in any case it would not have survived. According to Mallon, these copies were mostly written in 'common' script, in cursive capitals or in small letters, and it was the *ordinator* who transferred the text to the stone in square capitals. To corroborate his thesis, Mallon compared this procedure with that followed by some workshops of our own day; in particular, he studied an *atelier* in Algiers and published the documents bearing on the production of a tombstone inscription.[7]

It follows that the misunderstandings which can occur in the three different phases in the genesis of an inscription are to be sought, on the whole, in the passage from the 'common' script of the draft to the 'monumental' script of the provisional tracing on stone, and that the key to the interpretation of so many apparent oddities in epigraphy, of so many 'stonecutter's errors', is to be found almost exclusively in the manner of this passage. Here, too, is the key to a better dating of a text and to placing it in the graphic (and that means the cultural) environment in which it originated. In this way Mallon finally exonerates the cutter from the blame that generations of epigraphists have piled on him, since the cutter is now seen to be merely the one who physically executes what the *ordinator* has prepared for him. It is the *ordinator* who now bears the blame for everything: according to Mallon, rather like the compositor in our day.[8] It must be observed, however, that in printing the press reproduces exactly what the compositor has set, whereas the cutter may still modify what he finds, according to his own level of education. An incontrovertible result of Mallon's closely reasoned analysis is that very often a text destined for carving was drafted by someone basically devoid of any knowledge of monumental characters, or by someone who found it very difficult to produce the draft even in common script. Mallon, however, is less convincing when he tends to trace back various other peculiarities of an epigraphic text, such as interpuncts, apices, abbreviations, supralineates, to the written draft. Again, the presence of different characters and types of writing in the same text, even the style of writing and the layout—let us call it the 'page format'—of the text on the surface destined for the inscription: they are all explained by Mallon in this way. However, there is clearly nothing to object to in the observation that many 'errors' may have originated from the intervention of more than one hand in the *ordinatio* or from the process of dictation of the draft to the *ordinator*.[9]

The teaching of Mallon has been put to good use by a number of scholars, and especially by Spanish epigraphists who had worked for a long time in collaboration with Mallon. It may even be said that these Spanish scholars have adhered more closely to the subject proper to epigraphy, and that Mallon's work has been used by them in their further attempts to clarify and define the epigraphic document in its quality as a monument. In this respect, a most valuable work by Joaquín de Navascués[10] preceded some of Mallon's conclusions. Navascués insists on the fact that till now the linguistic aspect has attracted more attention than the palaeographic aspect, which has led to the danger of mistaking for a linguistic fact even what was a mere palaeographic misunderstanding. He makes the happy suggestion that use of the indexes of grammatical peculiarities in the epigraphic *corpora* might lead us to discover, even in the absence of a photographic reproduction or a facsimile, those texts which particularly call for palaeographic annotation. Navascués introduces genuinely new elements into the current state of research in Roman epigraphy, by taking into consideration—as for instance in the case of the inscriptions of the late Empire from Mérida—the totality of the epigraphic monument, and consequently the possibility of dating the text with the aid of numerous elements not merely internal or even exclusively palaeographic; of relying, for instance, on the help of the decorative elements. He also postulates, even though still somewhat imperfectly, the interdependence between epigraphic monument and funeral rite—and therefore also between the visible shape of the monument and the funerary equipment deemed necessary for those mysterious communications which take place after death—as well as the interdependence between the quality of the monument and the financial means of the deceased. (It should not be thought surprising that all our references should be exclusively to funerary texts, since in Roman epigraphy almost all available documents belong in this category.) For all these factors the approach used by Navascués is in the forefront of Roman epigraphic studies. The Spanish scholar did not go so far as openly to formulate the principle of the evaluation of the epigraphic monument as something determined by the desire of whoever commissioned it to communicate a message in durable form to his contemporaries and to posterity: a true monument for eternity, a genuine and conscious historiographical act on the part of an individual or of a community, as I put it a few years after Navascués' study.[11] I believe the reason for this limitation of his is to be found chiefly in the Spanish scholar's admirable caution in advancing new theories, and in his awareness of the difficulty of formulating new, yet objectively valid, concepts.

In the same year in which Navascués published his study, the great French epigraphist Louis Robert presented an embarrassing question at the opening of the Third International Congress of Greek and Latin Epigraphy in Paris: 'Nous sommes réunis ici entre épigraphistes,' said Robert. 'Mais qui sommes-nous?' Robert was anxious to specify that historians who distinguish between 'historically' valuable and 'historically' useless inscriptions may not be numbered among epigraphists; epigraphists are those, and only those, who believe in the intrinsic value of the inscription. An excessively abstract definition perhaps, but successful in making it clear that the point of view of the epigraphist is different from the palaeographer's.[12] It was Robert who later carried on a lively controversy with Mallon, claiming that for many epigraphists the methods suggested by the French palaeographer did not represent anything new: Salomon Reinach, according to Robert, had already taken into account, with regard to Greek inscriptions, the possibility of errors in the transcription from the original draft, but without achieving notable results, or at least without achieving results of such importance as to revolutionize the methods of Classical epigraphy. The controversy between Robert and Mallon[13] is embodied not only in specific passages but also in the continuous work done by Robert, through his *Bulletin épigraphique*, for the assessment of the inscription not only as palaeographic evidence, related almost exclusively to the development of writing, but in a wider, even if not always sufficiently defined, context. What is significant, anyhow, is Robert's approval of W. K. Pritchett's exhortation to find the extreme chronological limits of a phenomenon, even of a palaeographic phenomenon, and his similar approval of the similar ideas frequently expressed by Rehm and Wilhelm.[14] On the other hand it must be recognized that Mallon's warning not to resort too easily to an explanation in terms of a 'stonecutter's error' has been and is being reiterated with unflagging firmness by Italian epigraphists, such as Margherita Guarducci, Attilio Degrassi and Guido Barbieri. The controversy between Robert and Mallon, however, turns out to be partly pointless, if one considers the different fields of research to which the two French scholars refer. Mallon examines almost exclusively Roman texts, and we know that in the majority of cases these are funerary inscriptions, produced in local or peripheral workshops certainly not accustomed to making monuments requiring great skill or destined for great occasions. In these workshops, more easily than in others, the customer might bring along his own draft; sometimes he might even dictate his text or perhaps ask the workmen in the shop to compose it. That text would certainly be inelegant, drawn up in brief and undeveloped language, and would moreover often betray the effort to express in Latin what was usually thought, partly at least, in another language. In the vast orbit of the Mediterranean, of Roman Europe, of partially Romanized Asia and Africa, with countless substrata and diverse cultural *milieux*, there was also a simply boundless potential of phonetic material and its possible transcriptions. The comparison with the papyri, so profitably used by Mallon, is also dependent on this premise. Robert, on the other hand, derives his experience from Greek epigraphy, and especially from public texts, which are the choice product of the activity of the *polis*. They are composed in conformity with well-known formulas (discussed and repeated by many) in an environment culturally more homogeneous—even allowing for differences in dialect—and they are destined for a more attentive, more stable public, as is implicit in the character and structure of the *polis*, and therefore a public more inclined to meditate and remember. The error on the stone, which represents the major clue in Mallon's method—and a very precious clue—is therefore much less frequent in Greek communities. To sum up: with regard to the controversy between Mallon and Robert, we can only conclude with the calm but heartfelt words of Aristide Calderini,[15] which express the enthusiastic desire of a master of ancient scholarship for closer collaboration between papyrologists and epigraphists, between epigraphists and palaeographers. Mallon's approach, however, still retains all its validity; we have here a method which can lead to quite unexpected results, as recently in the case of the inscription of Zoe from Ragusa.[16]

A further, and in some respects definitive, step forward in the assessment of Roman inscriptions from the point of view of

B

writing, has been taken by Arthur and Joyce Gordon in their monumental recent collection of dated Latin inscriptions[17] and in their masterly *Contributions to the Palaeography of Latin Inscriptions*.[18] This work introduces with extraordinary clarity the principle of the distinction between the shape and the tracing of an engraved letter. With regard to the former, Mallon's views are basically accepted, i.e. that the *ordinator* is ultimately similar to the person writing with a pen, even if the *ordinatio* is often traced 'à pointe sèche' (Plate 1), and the study of the *ductus* can be pursued on a uniform basis for any kind of writing on any kind of material; on the other hand, the tracing, the manner and direction of the incision, the apices, any shape or mannerism directly due to the use of the chisel, anything that pertains to the last of the three stages described by Mallon (i.e. the cutting), and finally the way in which joins are effected (but only in their palaeographic, instrumental, aspect and not in their possible diplomatic implications)—all this is analysed autonomously and with unsurpassed skill. If Mallon's approach had apparently put the role of the stonecutter in the shade, the Gordons' studies have now exhaustively explored that area, and in this connection all we can do is to refer the reader to the rich dossier of case histories which they have assembled.[19]

II

THE TWO PHASES OF ENGRAVING

Since the publication of Mallon's work and of the Gordons', scholars have turned their attention to the possibility of deducing the technique and the phases in the genesis of a Roman inscription by examining the writing itself, the shape of the letters and the direction of the strokes. Earlier scholars had studied this problem mostly with reference to the terms and definitions in the ancient sources, which seem to indicate the technique and the phases of which we were speaking. To be sure, recent scholars have not given up this pursuit either, and it is therefore useful to sum up what knowledge we have of this subject.

Before we go any further, we must regretfully admit that we cannot assign any satisfactory Greek or Roman name to the written draft from which the *ordinator* is believed to have taken the text that had to be transferred to the stone in monumental writing: Mallon himself is content to use two French words, 'minute' and 'brouillon', though mostly the first.[20] On the surface at least, we are more fortunate with the two subsequent stages in the genesis of an inscription: the one which, following so many authoritative scholars, I have been describing as *ordinatio*, and the actual carving. It is evident that the tracking down of this practice in the ancient sources constitutes an irrefutable contribution to, and a valid corroboration of, the method followed in the direct analysis of epigraphic texts. In this respect the best-known source, as well as the most debated, is itself an inscription, namely, that shop-sign from Palermo which we have already mentioned.[21] It is worth while transcribing once more this bilingual Greek and Latin text:

ΣΤΗΛΑΙ	TITVLI
ΕΝΘΑΔΕ	HEIC
ΤΥΠΟΥΝΤΑΙ ΚΑΙ	ORDINANTVR ET
ΧΑΡΑΣΣΟΝΤΑΙ	SCVLPVNTVR
ΝΑΟΙΣ ΙΕΡΟΙΣ	AIDIBVS SACREIS
ΣΥΝ ΕΝΕΡΓΕΙΑΙΣ	CVM OPERVM
ΔΗΜΟΣΙΑΙΣ	PVBLICORVM

Kaibel[22] observed that most probably the person who composed this sign was neither Greek nor Roman (least of all Roman, I should say), since both texts reveal little familiarity with the two languages: especially in the Latin part the genitive *operum publicorum* (governed by *cum*) is simply copied *verbatim* from the magistrate's title *curator operum publicorum*. Perhaps the composer was a Carthaginian; this, however, is of no great importance, since (obviously) in a sign meant also for a public speaking Greek and Latin, the man displaying it must have been careful to use the most suitable technical terms. In fact, from the Latin part of the text we can extract two terms, *ordinare* and *sculpere*, with their Greek equivalents, which, however, no longer have any real significance for us. Actually, τυποῦν hardly corresponds to what we usually understand by *ordinare*. These terms could indeed refer to two different stages in the genesis of an inscription. We must remember that in other sources too, as we shall note further on, two distinct verbs (although *ordinare* is not one of them) are used to indicate in a general way the production or the setting up of an inscription; but above all we must observe that, whereas on the verb *sculpere* (in other sources *scalpere*) and on its meaning there is no room for argument, on the verb *ordinare* and on its meaning endless conjectures are possible. The reason is that before *scalpere* (or *sculpere*) many other sources in fact use the verb *scribere*. Naturally this involves another problem, which I shall discuss later, namely, whether there was a stage of *ordinatio* in the engraving of all or almost all Roman inscriptions, as Mallon, for example, categorically asserts,[23] or whether it was an almost exceptional or a merely partial procedure, as is maintained by Ferrua.[24] It seems obvious, at any rate, that *ordinare* indicates a genuinely separate stage in the genesis of an inscription, whether it amounts only to drafting the text or laying it out on the stone, or whether it includes the preliminary drawing on the stone, with the grid of the guidelines which, as a matter of fact, are to be found in almost all inscriptions. It is therefore possible to conclude with Mallon that the *ordinatio* consists in transferring the text on to the stone and giving it epigraphic form.[25]

The same twofold terminology, as in *ordinare* and *sculpere*, occurs, as we have said, in other epigraphic sources. To be precise, we read *scribere et sculpere* in three African inscriptions,[26] whereas in other texts—carefully collected by I. Calabi[27] —one of these same verbs is used in isolation, and they do not seem to indicate different stages in the work, but merely the order for an inscription (at times the customer uses one or the other of these verbs in the first person); or else they represent the signature of a shop: in this use we find *scribere, sculpere (scalpere), inscribere* or simply *facere*. Instances were already collected and annotated by Hübner.[28] The verb which is used most frequently in isolation is *scribere*, especially in signatures, in professional qualifications—*scriptor tituli*,[29] *scriptor titulorum*[30]—and in advertising signs, as for example in the unique group of painted inscriptions from Pompeii, where we read *scr(ipsit) Aemilius Celer*: that gentleman was *programmatum scriptor* (i.e. composed election posters), and he also took care to indicate his house (*Aemilius Celer hic habitat*) and to warn off those who erased his inscriptions (*invidiose qui deles aegrotes*).[31]

We also have evidence of one preparatory stage prior to the writing—very rare evidence, but in fact this stage is absolutely essential in the genesis of an inscription, even though Mallon could not take it into consideration; for it is outside the palaeographer's province and belongs to the epigraphist's proper sphere of interest. This stage consists in the preparation of the monument destined to contain the inscription and of the surface on which the text is to be inscribed. I am here referring to two rock inscriptions from Philippi, which give lists of the initiates of the cult of Silvanus.[32] On the first we read *P(ublius) Hostilius Philadelphus/ . . . titulum polivit/ de suo et nomina sodal(ium) inscripsit . . .*: in this text the preparation of the monument consists exclusively in the demarcation of the surface intended for the writing and in its polishing. The second text, on the other hand, also mentions the cutting of the rock to prepare the surface marked out for the writing and the dressing of that surface: *P(ublius) Hostilius P(ubli) l(ibertus) Philadelphus/ petram inferior(em) excidit et titulum fecit, ubi/ nomina cultor(um) scripsit et sculpsit . . .* In both inscriptions the term *titulus* indicates, not the writing, but the space properly dressed and intended for it. Generally speaking, it can be said that no other extant source prevents us from accepting so all-embracing a meaning for the word *titulus*: the meaning of 'inscription contained in its monumental setting'.

As can be seen, in the ancient sources the distinction between *ordinatio* and carving, as different stages in the production of an inscription, is not always clear; nevertheless—with all due reservations as to the actual operations covered by the first of these two words—such a distinction is sufficiently documented. We seem to have here a situation analogous to that of the Greek pottery workshops. We must remember, of course, that the painter himself chose the designs he would trace on the still rough surface of the vase; in this he was almost completely independent of the customer, and influenced only by the general preferences of the market. But in any case, the painter then signed the finished product by giving his name followed by the verb ἔγραψε; while the whole activity of the shop—the shaping of the vase, the colouring of the background, the baking—was ascribed to the owner (or to the foreman) whose name was followed by the common verb ἐποίησε.

More difficult still is the attempt to assign a name to the artisans who worked on the different stages of production, since the term *lapicida* seems to have been used for all the different functions. Varro says:[33] '*Qui lapides caedunt, lapicidas; qui ligna, lignicidas non dici*'; and by the term *caedunt* he means all the operations of stone-cutting, including, of course, also the preparation of the *titulus*. Sidonius Apollinaris, in a deservedly famous passage, attributes to the *lapicida* all the operations of writing as well, and goes so far as to use the term *quadratarius* too, for these same functions, introducing it into the sentence clearly for the sake of rhetorical variation:[34] . . . *sed vide ut vitium non faciat in marmore lapidicida* [sic]; *quod factum sive ab industria seu per incuriam mihi magis quam quadratario lividus lector adscribet*. And finally, Pliny the Elder uses the term *typus*, joined with the verb *scalpere*, to indicate a carved shape, perhaps including even a letter,[35] although *typus* is a noun of rather generic meaning.[36] Let me end by mentioning a conjecture, by now largely discarded, according to which the *ars characte-(raria)* mentioned in a Lyon inscription indicates precisely the art of the *lapicida*.[37]

III

WORKERS AND WORKSHOPS

The passage of Sidonius Apollinaris we have just quoted enables us to understand that it was not possible to use precise terms for the different artisans working in a stonemason's shop. Even today, when making arrangements for the funeral monument of a member of his family, an Italian will use the words 'scalpellino' or 'marmista' or—if he happens to remember his Classical studies—the word 'lapicida' for 'stonemason'. In the same way Sidonius Apollinaris said *lapidicida* (or *lapicida*) and *quadratarius* indifferently, even though he was aware, I imagine, that, taken literally, the two words had different meanings and referred to two different phases in the production of an inscription: *lapicida* is the man who handles the chisel or perhaps even the axe; *quadratarius* is, more precisely, the man who does the *ordinatio*, the one who skilfully prepares the surface for the inscription, i.e. puts in the margins, draws the marks for the alignment of the letters, figures out the proportions of each line and finally, according to Mallon's theory, draws on the stone the shape of the letters which the cutter will carve.

But, as we have seen, in practice it is not so: in spite of the formal analogy of which we spoke before, it would be useless to look in the ancient sources for evidence of a precise distinction between the workers engaged in the two stages just defined, a distinction such as we find in the production of Greek vases. Even in the case of important and valuable monuments it would be useless to look for the name, or rather the signature, of the *ordinator*, who ultimately is the same as the *quadratarius* (i.e. the man capable of transcribing a text from common script to monumental script, to square capitals); or for the name of the *lapicida*, that is, the owner of the shop in which the monument was produced. Even the expressions *scriptor tituli* and *scriptor titulorum*, of which we spoke earlier, are rare; besides, innumerable other sources provide other terms and they have the value of at least general evidence. What meaning could otherwise be ascribed to the definition which Petronius gives of Habinnas (. . . *sevir est idemque lapidarius qui videtur monumenta optime facere*)?[38] Sometimes instead of *lapidarius* we find *faber lapidarius*, without change of meaning; sometimes even *lapicidinarius*, a derivative of *lapicidina* or *lapidicina*, which meant stone quarry; sometimes *lapidecaesor*;[39] finally, in two inscriptions from Rome the same person is called *lapicida* and *scalptor*.[40] Again, we also find mention of *sculptores*, or more generically *artifices*, and (of course) of *quadratarii*. This last term is often used in apposition to *lapicidae* or *lapidarii*, and this helps us to understand that, as between these two nouns, *quadratarius* better defined the totality of the operations involved in the execution of an epigraphic monument,[41] from the squaring down of a cippus to the actual preparation and incision of a stone surface. On one occasion, in an inscription from Rome, the term *quadratari* is followed by an apposition which unfortunately is incomplete, since the stone itself is broken,[42] but which, in my opinion, could be restored [*qua*]*dratari a m*[*armore*], perhaps to distinguish the artisans of a stonemason's shop from those who, in Rome more than elsewhere, turned out painted inscriptions on *alba*, on *tabulae* or on whitewashed walls. For we should not forget that while in every city there was the custom we see in Pompeii, of painting commercial advertisements and electoral slogans on walls, in Rome a great deal of additional work was done writing legal texts meant to be displayed in public and afterwards deposited in the *tabularium*. This would show even more effectively that there was no precise distinction of functions, at least in the sense meant by Mallon, between *ordinatores* and cutters within the same workshop, but that a distinction more readily developed between those who worked in stone and those who worked with more perishable materials, such as wood or paint. In practice, then, the genesis of an inscription on stone amounts to a far more complex and fragmented series of operations than Mallon believes; his deductions, however, remain no less valid since, as I said, he speaks as a palaeographer, and from the palaeographic point of view he has appraised inscriptions correctly.

Sometimes the artisan in a stonemason's shop is also referred to by the more generic term *marmorarius*;[43] this indicates that it must have been rare indeed for a shop to specialize exclusively in lapidary writing, but that, more appropriately, inscriptions were executed in shops equipped for general stone work, although, as a rule, not for really high-class sculpture. We are helped once more, however, by a shop sign. Here is the text of an inscription from Rome, now in the *Galleria Lapidaria* in the Vatican:[44]

D M

TITVLOS   SCRI

BENDOS   VEL

SI   QVID   OPE

RIS   MARMOR

ARI   OPVS   FV

ERIT   HIC   HA

BES

It is fair to suppose that, generally speaking, many other types of monuments could be produced in the same workshop where inscriptions were made: for example, the *tabulae lusoriae*,[45] especially those for the game of *latrunculi*, which had to be prepared very accurately in a precise geometric design, so that the finished product should exhibit a perfect checkerboard lightly carved on the surface. Sun dials, very common everywhere in antiquity, were another type of monument where an engraver could display his skill in tracing very thin lines in a geometrically perfect pattern.[46] Lastly, the same workshop would also turn out the ornamental elements of an epigraphic monument, such as the mouldings, which often consisted of a series of parallel incised lines, which we may call 'border trenches' and which are very common in low-priced Roman funerary monuments from the end of the second Christian century; although in some Western provinces—in Gaul, for example—they seem to have been in use since the first century, especially to frame ornamental reliefs, as in the triumphal arch at Orange and in other monuments in Narbonensis. In other cases, a recessed panel was prepared to receive the inscription. This produced the effect of making the ornamental parts not thus treated stand out in relief—parts such as the moulding around the edges and the pediment,[47] the decorative motifs on the tympanum—rosettes, pateras, gorgons' heads, dolphins, goblets, etc.—and also any figured reliefs that were integral parts of the monument, either because they were (as so often) set on the same surface as the inscription, or because they were indispensable for completing the conceptual meaning of the written text. Sometimes, as the archaeologist well knows, these reliefs represent tasks performed by the deceased during his lifetime—and we are here speaking above all of funerary monuments, since sculptures of a religious or political character were usually the work of differently equipped shops; or else they represent symbolic objects or *genre* scenes. At this point another problem can arise. We can ask: what were the stages in the preparation of a monument that contained both figured ornamentation and inscription; in other words, what was usually mass-produced and what was custom-made to meet the customer's specifications? But this will be discussed later on, since it also involves the problem of what the *ordinatio* of a text really means.

Bronze letters, or, at any rate, metal letters, destined for *inscriptiones caelatae* and prepared in a foundry from permanent moulds, were the only exception to the normal procedure for the execution of an inscription within a stonemason's shop. It follows, therefore—and this is important for dating inscriptions produced by this technique—that metal letters, whose moulds were kept and used over a long period of time, to a large extent escaped the effects of both palaeographic evolution and changing chisel techniques, i.e. of the general development of the letters concerned. For this reason, as well as because of the typically monumental character of these texts (which tend more than others towards archaic forms), the inscriptions on rostra or similar structures, or on epistyles of temples and arches—most often executed in metal letters—are to be dated almost exclusively through the historical or institutional data contained in the text itself, rather than through our knowledge of epigraphic writing.[48] On the other hand, it is obvious that small metal letters, such as the *utere felix* set on belts as ornamental bosses, were far less likely to escape the evolution of the letter-forms concerned. Mosaic inscriptions are something different again: they were executed in the same workshops in which the mosaic floor was assembled; in fact, the artisan here found the *ordinatio* of the text to be included made much easier by his habit of exactly framing the space to be used for the tessellated pattern, and of subdividing it according to very precise rules.[49] Entirely different, clearly, and not closely related to the activities of the stonemason's shop, is the case of the *scriptores* of painted inscriptions, who probably had their own separate *ateliers*, like the *Aemilius Celer* of Pompeii, whom we met before. It must have been very rare indeed—at least, it is not easy to envisage it—for monumental inscriptions (that is to say, inscriptions not meant to disappear at the first whitewash) to be painted rather than carved. On the other hand, we must not forget that both in the Greek and in the Roman world (as indeed today) the interiors of temples and of hypogea (like those of the Etruscans) had large painted panels with legends also painted; but, being thus placed, they were protected against both men and the weather. Lastly, we must also remember that on large amphorae of Greek and especially of Roman manufacture some marks of origin or capacity were painted under a glaze strong enough to resist both wear and tear and corrosion by salt water.

A stonemason's shop—or we might more effectively and comprehensively call it *officina*, a term already used in anti-quity[50]—thus developed a special monumental style, and this style could not but influence, and in turn be influenced by, that of inscriptions on stone. The artisans were the same, whether they worked on the mouldings, the sculptured reliefs or the lettering, though perhaps each of them might specialize in one activity more than in the others; in fact, often enough the same man did the entire work. The instruments, as we shall see, were the same; the stone they put their hand to was the same; and the same, too, were the customers they had to please, now with an adjective in the text, now with a special symbol in the orna-mentation. In the attempt to trace back, to reconstruct, the 'language' (as it were) of such an *officina*, few elements are as precious as the discarded fragments in the store-rooms of our museums, the items which normally swell the number of 'rejects' in the cellars or are hidden away among the bushes of ornamental courtyards and in overcrowded museum gardens. Our modern stonemasons' establishments, located near our cemeteries, offer no parallel, for, as a rule, they carve exclu-sively on plaques or on slabs: stone sheets too thin to allow for the growth of a genuine 'language' of funerary monuments.

It is interesting to imagine what such an ancient stonemason's *officina* might have looked like. Fortunately, one or two have at times come to light and have provided those precious pieces— barely sketched in, or still unfinished, or just ready for inscribing—which are so useful for our understanding of what *ordinatio* actually involved. They have been found in Rome, Ostia and Pompeii.[51] We are better off for painted and sculptured scenes, in which we see a *marmorarius* at work; but he is always merely shown busy with unspecified work on a monument, as Blümner's still useful survey makes clear,[52] and these representations add nothing to our knowledge of the details of the trade—not even as regards the way in which the *scalprum* or the *malleus* was held, not to mention the actual shape of these instruments. Worthy of mention among these representations is one from an *aedicula* in Bordeaux,[53] the rock sculpture on Mount Hymettus[54]—the only one of them showing an inscribed monument—and a miniature in the Vatican manuscript of Vergil.[55] We remain equally uninformed about the life and the trade organization of those engaged in the *ars lapidaria*,[56] unless we want to bring up once more the hypothesis that they were incorporated in the guild of *fossores*,[57] and to stress again the close links, both technical and economic, which existed between stonemasons' shops and stone quarries.[58]

IV

STONES, TOOLS AND THEIR INTERACTION

The supply of the stone required for monuments and the problems connected with it must have had a direct and considerable influence on the activities of the stonemasons' shops as well as on the cost of the finished product. Unfortunately we are not well informed on this subject.[59] It is worth noting that in the processes of hewing the stone from the quarry, of numbering the blocks destined for use in accordance with an overall design, or of any other kind of numbering or checking, various letters and numbers were often cut into the stone. These marks served an exclusively practical purpose, yet quite often were not erased from the finished monument.[60] It is not improbable, too, that in some instances a figure for an estimate of costs was transcribed from the draft to the monument.[61] Naturally, all these problems did not arise when the inscription was cut directly on a natural rock, after a suitable surface had been polished and prepared, as in the case of the inscriptions in the sanctuary of Silvanus at Philippi, mentioned above (p. 12), as well as of many others: let us note, in particular, the milestone at Donnaz, in the Aosta Valley, hewn, together with its base and a scotia, directly out of the cliff face[62]—an example, very rare in the Roman world, of a monument carved out of the rock at the precise spot where it was to be set up. This instance is indeed an exceptional one, much more so than among the Greek and other Eastern cultures. Among the Persians, the Armenians and the Parthians, for example, rock inscriptions extolling a monarch were cut on high peaks and were addressed exclusively to the gods. The Romans—even if at first sight this statement might seem an over-simplification—addressed their monuments, especially those set up by individuals, to an endless posterity. Funeral monuments lined the highways, and this above all else, even more than ancestor cult, helped to keep the past before the eyes of generations ever on the move.

This must also be kept in mind if we are to understand the reason why in Roman monuments an almost exclusively frontal view predominates. With this problem we shall deal later. But while discussing stones and the preparation of blocks (*lapides quadrati*) for carving, we cannot help remarking that almost all Greek monuments are well polished on every side, and even the back, though not polished, is at least smoothed down, especially in the fifth and fourth centuries—less so later, during the late Hellenistic period, mostly as a consequence of new concepts in architecture and town planning. On the other hand, Roman monuments—in particular stelae, altars and funeral cippi—are sometimes barely roughed out at the back; as for the sides, if they are not made into panels with mouldings framing them, they quite plainly show the marks of the chisel or—during the late Empire—those of the claw. In some instances even the front is polished only in the portion that bears the inscription, while the rest is only roughed out with the chisel, and at times this even encroaches on the inscribed panel; and this is true even for monuments of fairly good work-manship both in appearance and in the quality of the lettering. One of the clearest examples of this practice is a stele from Amsoldingen,[63] now in the Thun Museum. Another is an imperial dedication from Modena,[64] where the surface is polished down to the lower guideline of the last line of text,

PLATES

I. FRAGMENT OF INSCRIPTION (UNPUBLISHED) FROM RUBIERA, IN THE *TERRITORIUM* OF REGIUM LEPIDI

Note the traced guidelines, both horizontal and vertical, and the clear evidence of an *ordinatio* of the text itself in the (erroneous) first incision of the S in the first line. The letters O and D are drawn with the aid of compasses

II. ARCHAEOLOGICAL MUSEUM, REGGIO EMILIA

Funerary stele of a *marmorarius*, showing the principal tools of his trade

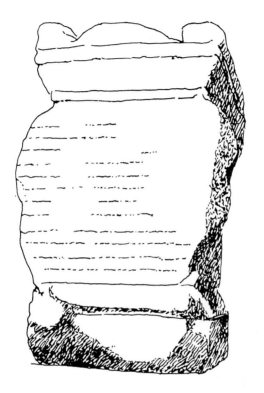

III. MUSEUM, BATH (AQUAE
SULIS). SMALL ROMAN ALTAR,
PREPARED FOR RECEIVING AN
INSCRIPTION

IV. COLOSSO COLLECTION, UGENTO. FUNERARY CIPPUS

The stonecutter has clearly taken little notice of the traced guidelines

V. ARCHAEOLOGICAL MUSEUM, LECCO. PART OF FUNERARY STELE FROM PORTO CESAREO

The guidelines fan out slightly to the right

VI. RUDIAE. FUNERARY STELE

The preparation of the panel here included three
equidistant vertical lines

but no further, with the rest of the panel intended for the inscription (which is framed by a cornice) left unpolished.

As a rule, during the process of *ordinatio*, the polished space is entirely marked out with guidelines, even where it must have been assumed that the inscription would not require them all; and this is again important evidence for the complexity and diversity of operations in producing an inscription within a stonemason's shop.

As we have seen, the value of the stone used for inscriptions is a very important factor; this depended not only on the cost of quarrying and transporting it, but also on its natural quality, which, however, might take second place to numerous technical considerations, as well as to the fashion of the moment. That in Rome, at least down to the time of the Gracchi, tuff (*peperino*) was used almost exclusively is due not only to the proximity of tuff quarries, but also to the persistence of the 'graffito' technique, which was no longer employed for graffiti as such (these were executed by means of a hard and sharp point), but for incised lettering. As we shall see later, the chisel was used (although less and less towards the end of the Republican period) to broaden and rectify the graffito cutting (probably done with a thick pointed instrument), or to cut directly into the surface at a right angle, to produce a rounded, U-shaped incision (∪) or a rough, irregular 'string' cut (∪ or similarly). The introduction of the V-section trench, produced directly by means of the chisel, by cutting down obliquely towards the vertex of the angle at the bottom of the trench from two incisions on the surface, truly revolutionized epigraphic writing and made possible the use of harder stones such as travertine and—with increasing frequency from the beginning of the Principate—marble from Luni.[65] Soft stones, however, continued to be popular because they were easier to work and hence less expensive: anyone could use them, even an amateur or a common scribe, as I have

c

shown in the large collection of inscriptions from the Salentine peninsula.[66] All the sandstones belong in this category; while for monuments that had to be durable without being particularly valuable, limestones with more or less developed crystal structure were preferred. Very hard stone, such as Euganean trachyte, was used for products meant to withstand a great deal of wear and tear, such as some road surfaces and some milestones. Undoubtedly the analysis of the stone is a good criterion for establishing the provenance of an inscription, whenever there is good reason to think that it has been moved from its original place. If, however, costly marble is involved, the intentions and the purpose (*animus*) of the customer must be taken into account: perhaps he regarded the monument as so important as to require suitably precious material. At times, too, the difference between the stone used for the inscription and the material used for the monument of which it forms part can give a clue as to the intentions and ideas of the person who planned the monument. Finally, petrological analysis can obviously help in dating a text, whenever we know with precision in what period the quarry producing that particular stone was in use.[67]

The difficulties involved in obtaining the stone necessary for monuments and for all other social needs help to explain why some inscribed stones were reused for a new text—a frequent occurrence from the third century A.D.[68]—and why persons violating tombs were threatened with such severe penalties, especially from the end of the second century; although the possibility remains that tomb robbers were also after valuables buried with the dead. Repeated inscriptions—that is to say, texts carved twice—represent a separate problem. If, as so often, the second text is opisthographic, i.e. is engraved on the back of the same stone, it is nearly always a corrected version of the first, either because there were obvious mistakes in the first, or because its workmanship was so poor that the customer complained.[69] If, on the other hand, identical or almost identical texts are found on separate stones, distant from one another, homonymy (which is not rare) coupled with widespread use of stereotyped formulae must be the answer. This possibility also exists in the case of verse inscriptions, i.e. of tombstone epigrams; for there can be no doubt that collections of such verses were put at the disposal of the customer by the more elegant and better equipped establishments.[70]

We have seen that the use of a particular type of stone can depend not only on the availability of the stone itself, on the prevailing economic conditions and on the fashion of the times, but also on the available techniques in using the tools of the trade. We have three ways of gathering information on the use of the *scalprum* (the chisel) on stone, but all three do not suffice to give us precise data. First, we have a few tools of this type kept in museums and collections, especially along the *limes* in Germany and in the Danubian region; but there is no evidence that any of these was ever used for epigraphic writing in particular. Next, there is useful information in the numerous representations of such tools on Roman reliefs, especially on funerary monuments: on the stele shown in Plate 2 there appear both the *scalprum* and the *malleus* (the hammer), also the tools required for the squaring of the stone, the *asciae* and *dolabrae*,[71] plus tools also used by architects, such as squares, compasses, levels. Actually, these tools are very seldom meant to represent the profession of the deceased, or to accompany him symbolically on his last journey;[72] almost always, and especially from the third century A.D., they suggest the concept of the inviolability of the tomb, symbolized chiefly by the *ascia*, the first tool the mason used on the fresh and still shapeless block of stone.[73] There have been endless discussions about the meaning of this symbol and about its origin; at present, scholars tend to ascribe it to Dalmatian influences dating from the first Christian century. Personally, I am of the opinion that the *ascia* is the visual expression of the tool abandoned on the tomb at the moment of completion—abandoned because, together with the tomb itself, it has become sacred to the chthonic deities, just as the plough used to trace the boundaries of a new city was sacred, or the boundary stone set to delimit a religious enclosure or a dedicated area. The strong chthonic sentiment, which pervades Roman religion and is so deeply rooted in Etruscan origins, led to belief in the release of the *manes* from the underworld and in the *devotio* of whatever had had a share in opening a passage to the kingdom of the dead. Analogous magical significance also invested the symbols, whether monstrous or phallic, which workmen set in a newly built curtain wall.

From the extant specimens and from visual representations we can reconstruct two types of *scalprum*: one with straight edge and one that may be called 'nib-pointed'.[74] A third source of useful data is provided by the marks of the chisel strokes, often still visible inside the incision. As a rule, at least in more ambitious monumental inscriptions, the marks of the strokes were eliminated by careful polishing *ad unguem*; yet sometimes, with a good magnifying lens, it is still possible to discern them. From these elements it is also possible to reconstruct the *ductus* and to determine the degree of inclination of the instrument to the line of writing.[75] The use of the *scalprum* for the 'finishing strokes' added to the letters, i.e. for the apices and other decorative strokes, has been exhaustively described by the Gordons.[76] But much research is still needed on the shape of this instrument and on the different varieties of it used to obtain different strokes. Above all, we must aim to collect data in such quantity as to make valid classifications possible; there is a need for an archaeologist–epigraphist who would devote to the *scalprum* the attention which L. W. Jones and so many other palaeographers have devoted to the *punctorium* of the medieval scribes.

In a way, we are better informed on the various shapes of the *malleus*: this instrument, however, never came into contact with the surface of the stone.[77] For some inscriptions, and especially for the tablets of the *columbaria* and the plaques on cinerary urns, the drill was sometimes used, from the second half of the second century A.D. It was also used for circular interpuncts, but these are rare; this is one of the few cases where interpuncts can help to date a text, since all the other forms—triangles (sometimes very acute-angled), ivy or palm leaves, arrows, or the shapes of a V or Z—are in use more or less indifferently and even alternate at any given period.[78] (Another exception is the square or rectangular interpunct, copied from the epigraphic practice of the late Hellenistic period and used, especially, in Roman inscriptions in Greece and Macedonia of the Republican period.)

We can be sure that compasses were also to be found among the tools of the stonemason's shop, in particular during the late Republic and in the Augustan period. At times it is still possible to detect the tiny hole at the centre of an O or of a Q, where the *ordinator* had inserted the point of the compass to draw the letter (Plate 1). Quite often the C too was produced by cutting half of a circle, the remaining half of which is still faintly visible, and then continuing from the stopping-points along the top and bottom guidelines. In one instance (not isolated, of course) the cutter by mistake cut the entire circle: the result was a LVOILIA instead of LVCILIA.[79] Such errors are due to both carelessness and ignorance, phenomena that we shall discuss later on. The S also, though less frequently, may be produced by juxtaposing, one above the other, two small circles. An example of this method is provided by the monumental inscriptions of the mausolea of the Murcii in Sarsina,[80] but the same could be shown in many other cases. Compasses were also used to mark out openings at the top or bottom of letters. In particular, they were used to define the shape of the letter V and also of A and M; the latter, especially in rather archaic inscriptions, looks like two V's turned upside down and joined together. The existence, for some letters, of cut-out patterns made of either wood or metal cannot be ruled out,[81] but in all probability the square and the compass were the cutter's whole equipment. These tools were also used to work out the module of each line;[82] for the module can present much variety within the same Roman inscription, and the result is a design effect quite different from the essential monotony of module in Greek inscriptions, even those belonging to the best Hellenistic period.

We have already noted that Roman epigraphic technique was entirely revolutionized when very hard stones came into use: on this type of stone a V-section trench was used, and this favoured the development of lettering away from the archaic forms, which were themselves derived from the primitive 'graffito' writing and therefore consisted of geometric strokes— the only ones that can be produced with a stylus held with wrist and forearm necessarily rigid.[83] The 'string' cut, with straight sides and rounded section, continued in use even when the V-section trench had become established: that is to say, throughout the second century of the Christian era. This method is quite common in Greek inscriptions, where the small size of the letters made it necessary to use a chisel which cut the surface of the stone exactly in the centre of the trench (though the edges could later be enlarged and polished) rather than at its edges. In the Etruscan and Italic inscriptions, especially in those from the territory of the Paeligni and the Messapii, this technique survived down to the first century B.C., and longer still, especially for low-priced monuments, in those regions where a porous and volcanic stone was used. Contrary to what scholars have maintained hitherto,[84] the V-shaped trench was thus not in use until lapidary writing became widespread, and its introduction—quite slow and not contemporaneous in all areas and establishments—marked the beginning of the development of real calligraphy, which culminated in the 'shaded' letters that came into use in the middle of the first century B.C.[85] and in the development of serifs (as the Gordons call them). As a consequence, however, the practice of filling the cuttings with colouring matter—black or red, sometimes even gold—fell into disuse. As for the question whether the painting of letters in inscriptions was in common use, I incline towards a negative answer: the extant specimens are exceedingly few, whereas on the Etruscan urns the traces of colour are clearly visible to this day. The 'string' cut, on the other hand, continued to be the practice for bronze lettering. One might say that in the development of monumental epigraphy the effect of light replaced the effect of colour—a new experiment with light-and-shade techniques to be added to those already known to us from the Hellenistic baroque and connected with that other innovation, the change of module in the lettering from one line to the next within the same inscription.

In some particularly fine epigraphic work—especially in religious dedications and honorary inscriptions—the edges of the actual cut are rounded off[86] and polished with great care, truly *ad unguem*, right down to the end of the third century of the Christian era.

V

THE PREPARATION OF THE PANEL

Many scholars have emphasized the importance of 'unfinished' epigraphic monuments: Cagnat himself discussed the subject at length[87] and more recently Mallon returned to it,[88] placing the incomplete texts on the same level as those containing obvious errors of transcription; for him, the 'unfinished' and the 'error' provide glimpses into the real nature of *ordinatio*. With their help we can single out those errors which, originating in the *ordinator*'s misunderstanding of the written draft, prevent us, in the case of inscriptions on stone, from observing at first hand the same phenomena of evolution as in common script, and thus from inserting inscriptions into a palaeographic context common to texts on papyrus and other non-durable materials.

It is undeniable that a monument left unfinished, perhaps even still found in the shop, as has been the case by mere accident, not only in Pompeii, but also in Rome and in Ostia,[89] makes it possible for us to glimpse some unsuspected features of the production process, or to confirm about other features what till then were mere conjectures. I must confess that, face to face with the marble crater with Athena and Marsyas in the National Museum in Athens,[90] which is in fact unfinished, or with the funeral chapel in the Antiquario comunale in Rome, with its 'unfinished' portraits,[91] I had precisely this feeling—the sensation of being able to recapture something,

the immediacy of which would otherwise have been irretrievably lost; at the risk of seeming excessively romantic, I will say
that the very mark left by the chisel seemed to me fresher, and
the marble or the limestone seemed to show its open wounds,
without the healing touch of the hand polishing it *ad unguem*.
Accordingly, 'unfinished' texts, like those mentioned by
Cagnat and Mallon,[92] arouse our interest in an extraordinary
manner, because they offer the justified hope of capturing a
'provisional', an 'intermediate' element, enabling us to understand the actual course of the work going on within the large
officina, or within the four—or perhaps eight—walls of the
smaller shop. At this point we must distinguish different cases:
there are unfinished inscriptions where the letters still uncut are
already traced with a point or in paint,[93] that is to say,
inscriptions still carrying the obvious traces of a complete
ordinatio, and there are those the unfinished part of which
presents no such evidence; and again, in the latter category, we
must distinguish between those for which we can conjecture an
ordinatio done with chalk or charcoal, which have left no
traces,[94] and those for which there was no *ordinatio* at all, as we
must surmise in order to explain the complete absence of traces
in that part of the stone where the cutting, for whatever reason,
was not done. But we must also determine whether the text is
only apparently incomplete, for the cutter may have mis-
understood the original, or else he may have kept on carving,
mechanically (as it were), out of the habit of writing a stereotyped formula.[95] Consequently, in order to profit by the 'unfinished' inscription, we must first examine the surface very
carefully and establish to which of the preceding categories a
particular text belongs. Nor can we ever entirely eliminate the
possibility that in the sections apparently clean and without
incision or traces of *ordinatio* there may have been at one time
an outline drawn with charcoal or chalk.

   This problem, itself quite serious, entails another: whether there always was an *ordinatio* of the text to be carved. Mallon maintains that there was an *ordinatio* at all times and that some shapeless stubs which are to be seen next to the chisel, the axe or the hammer in representations of stonemasons' workshops are to be interpreted as chalk and charcoal.[96] Not without justification Ferrua has firmly rejected his hypothesis[97] and has expressed the opinion that chalk or charcoal was used exclusively to jot down the text on the stone as a memo and not as a graphic model. He points to the example of some catacomb inscriptions on which, either below or next to the carved lettering, painted lettering is still visible. Against this, I should like to suggest that this may be a case of 'reinforcing' the painted inscription by incision. This would be easy to understand, since catacombs were much more frequented than the funerary vaults or the *columbaria* of the pagan world. There, painted inscriptions, after the Etruscan model, are commonly found side by side with carved ones. In the catacombs, however, painting can disappear more easily, owing to contact with the air and the effects of the smoke of the torches. More convincing, perhaps, is Ferrua's opinion that those shapeless stubs are not, as Mallon thinks, chalk or charcoal, but chisels of a particular type, short and with points of different sizes, such as (I would add) we can still see in some workshops in the Alps or Apennines, but no longer in the urban shops near our cemeteries, where the electric drill reigns supreme.

Ferrua, therefore, maintains that *ordinatio* was rare, and in fact done only for more important inscriptions. This is too extreme a conclusion and, at least for pagan inscriptions, it is not corroborated by what can be observed in the majority of texts. Personally I am of the opinion that there was an *ordinatio* (if we use the term in a very wide sense) in at least ninety per cent of cases; it still remains to establish, however, what it actually involved and through what phases and operations it was effected. For example, we must accept that in almost all cases guidelines were traced; for we find such lines—even if only with the help of strong lights skimming the surface—in nearly every case. Where we do not see them, we are entitled to think that in all probability they were drawn with varnish or minium, or that perhaps a taut string was used—unless, of course, our text is slipshod in execution and devoid of any real attempt at layout. How else, in fact, could we explain that passage from Persius: ... *scit tendere versum/ non secus ac si oculo rubricam dirigat uno*?[98] Later on, Ferrua himself clarifies his position and helps us to define the problem in a more satisfactory manner by stating that where there are guidelines there was no *ordinatio*, since, in his opinion, a text cannot be partly traced with a sharp point and partly drawn with chalk or charcoal. This last remark cannot be accepted, first of all because, as we have seen, the guidelines could be merely painted, but also because in fact we have here two separate operations, one the tracing of the guidelines, and one the drawing of the text. Actually, we must agree on the precise meaning of the term *ordinatio*: are the guidelines part of it or not? Ferrua says they are not, but then he goes on to admit that the tracing of the guidelines and the drawing of the text are simultaneous or at least closely related operations, since both must be effected with the same tool. Ferrua has opened the door to a wider criticism of Mallon and in particular of Mallon's contention that nearly all the elements of composition in an inscription, such as the formal structure of the text and its layout, are to be ascribed to the original written draft.

We must distinguish clearly—or, I should perhaps say, we must admit the possibility of a distinction—between an earlier stage in the preparation of the text (or rather, of the monument), prior to the transcription, and the transcription itself; and the latter too would require tools, and would follow a routine, to some extent independent of the suggestions in the written draft.[99] This distinction is tantamount to recognizing several different phases and factors in the genesis of an inscription. It is unavoidable, not only because numerous 'unfinished' monuments provide evidence for such phases, but also because it is impossible entirely to separate the inscription from its monumental setting. To do so would mean to approach the problem from the point of view of palaeography—as Mallon did, deliberately, and with valid methods and convincing conclusions—but not from the point of view of epigraphy.

A question arises at the outset: whether, at the time when the customer first put in his order, the monument—nearly always a funerary one—was still all in the future, a mere *lapis quadratus*, at the most squared down to the size most commonly in demand for its purpose; or whether it was already equipped with structural and decorative elements, with a polished inset for the inscription and with the more fashionable figurative symbols. To this question there can be no single answer valid for all cases; on each occasion the epigraphist will have to search carefully for the traces of different stages of work and of their sequence. The opinions I am going to express here are merely a general summary based on long observation and are valid only as a formula necessarily subject to adaptation.

As I said before, there are examples of 'unfinished' monuments completely provided with all the structural and decorative elements of their day, but without the inscription itself. For unknown reasons, they have come down to us in the state in which they were before our hypothetical customer came into the shop with his text, or dictated or explained the desired text to the shop's scribe, or else before the *ordinator* (it would perhaps be better to call him the *scriptor*) transferred the text to the stone, and the mason—the real stonecutter this time, with his actual chisel and hammer—engraved it. There are such monuments in the museums, albeit few. An example may be seen in the Archaeological Museum at Pola: a tall stele ornamented with pilasters topped by small capitals with leaf decorations, with volutes around the pediment and a little gorgon's head on the tympanum. More common are monuments of smaller size, mere small cippi, so that we cannot be certain that they were ever meant to be inscribed: perhaps they were only intended as anonymous marks over a tomb or, more probably, at the corners of a burial plot. This was fairly common in Greece, especially for slaves' burials, as is abundantly shown by the numerous instances in the Ceramicus. These, then, would not be 'unfinished' products: with a rosette at the front or, in the case of Roman cippi, simply with an *advocatio* to the *Dei Manes*, they were complete and ready for use. It is possible that in some cases such a cippus, perhaps while still in the shop, was used for the inscription of a complete text: this is probably what happened in the case of a monument from Brindisi,[100] where (except for the first line, with only the *praenomen* of the deceased) the text is placed well below the dedication to the *Dei Manes*, which by itself, in two lines, occupies one third of the inscribed surface.

In other cases the state of the 'unfinished' work is far less advanced. In some Greek funerary stelae and in a great many Roman ones the tympanum shows a rough circular ornament, which could easily be turned into a flower, a star, a wheel, a *patera*, or even a gorgon's head. We can see examples of this class in the Archaeological Museum at Fiesole. Apparently the customer had not expressed any particular preference with regard to this ornament, and the price he was prepared to pay did not suffice to complete the work. Much the same can be said for a very interesting category of funeral monuments: the sarcophagi which became fashionable in the Western part of the Empire from the second century onwards. Often the lateral panels and even some sections of the front, most frequently those flanking the inscribed inset, are nothing but projecting, rough-hewn surfaces, waiting to be completed with some relief-work, which, however, was never done. As examples of this we have the splendid sarcophagi of the *Lapidario Estense* at Modena. Finally, in some cases the monument appears complete, not only in its structural features, but also in its portraiture; it is, therefore, not unreasonable to think that on some funerary stelae even the portraits were 'ready-made' and required only the addition of (at most) some distinctive detail. Ultimately this confirms what has always been thought, that iconography, outside the field of popular tradition, was influenced by official portraiture and closely followed its course of development. It is in this way that we must explain a stele in the Antiquarium at Tihany in Hungary: the portraits on this stele have hair-styles of the time of Trajan, and there is a large decorated panel; but the panel for the inscription, suitably placed in its full monumental setting, is blank. Obviously we are here in the presence of mass-production of monuments of a common type: it was from this range, as far as it was stocked by the workshop, that the customer in the first place made his choice. The phenomenon is not a new development in the Roman world, and, like many others, it originates in Etruscan practice. We find, in fact, that the Etruscans mass-produced sarcophagus lids and at times fitted a lid on a sarcophagus of very different size. This practice, alongside the production of actual sarcophagi, continued in Etruria throughout the Roman period.

As a generalization, we may say that the preparation of the figures and symbols nearly always preceded the engraving of the text. This is proved by those monuments in which the inscription looks squashed, compressed between a decorative motif and the border,[101] in a space that had not been meant for it; by those in which the letters carefully skip over the sculptured symbols and occupy what available space there is, as in the Bologna stele of a L. Statorius Bathyllus, where lettering is placed around the compass and the level;[102] and finally, by those in which part of the border has been chiselled out to make room for the text, not always because the writer or the cutter had left something out. On the other hand, there are a few monuments in which the border was added after the cutting of the letters: this was done by chiselling down the level of the epigraphic inset all round, except where the text overruns its allotted space and covers part of the area intended for the border.[103] There are also examples of work done concurrently on the inscription and on the figurative elements, sometimes at the expense of the former, which comes to be partially mutilated by the finishing touches added to the latter.[104]

On the 'unfinished' (i.e. uninscribed) monuments, the inset panel is nearly always already provided with lines, in readiness for a future text. This proves that the guidelines were the responsibility of the mason who had worked on the rest of the stele. It is likely that in cases where this is not so the guidelines were later drawn with a cord covered with vermillion. But since guidelines are to be seen on almost all epigraphic monuments, it is obvious that they were regularly incised during the first stage of preparation of the monument, the stage which we have just been discussing and which we shall call 'workshop preparation', reserving the term *ordinatio*—whose vagueness in the ancient sources has been sufficiently stressed above—for one of the subsequent stages. One of the most significant examples of Roman monuments not yet inscribed, but with cut guidelines well in evidence, is a small altar now kept in the Archaeological Museum at Bath (Aquae Sulis) (Plate 3).

Other evidence further corroborates the conclusion that the guidelines were traced independently of the prospective text. There are, for example, numerous inscriptions in which the last lines of the text go beyond the end of the guidelines: the engraving shows the effect of this and the letters tend to stray all over.[105] More often it is the guidelines that go beyond what is needed for the text. At other times the cutter pays scant attention to them and carves letters either taller or much smaller than the module provided for by the lines (Plate 4).[106] It is even worse when the guidelines are not drawn straight and either all slant to one side or fan out progressively (Plate 5): if the cutter follows them, the final effect is rather disconcerting.[107] In some shops, lack of skill on the part of an artisan has given rise to numerous instances of the same irregularity, such as the slightly, but consistently, tilted axis of some texts at Forum Cornelii.[108]

The most correct method of tracing guidelines is represented by 'rails': pairs of parallel lines traced at a constant distance from each other, the top 'rail' supporting one line of writing from below, the bottom 'rail' crowning the next line from above, so that they delimit the spaces between the lines. Between pairs of these 'rails', we often find another parallel line traced along the middle of the line of writing. This was meant for the horizontal strokes of particular letters,[109] such as the cross strokes of A and H, the middle strokes of E and F and the joins of the curved strokes in B, G, P and R. Finally, we have examples of vertical strokes traced to subdivide the face of the panel into squares. The strokes of some letters lean on these verticals; or, as in an inscription from Rudiae, they fix the place for the point of the compasses used to trace an ornamental circle on the pediment (Plate 6; cf. Plate 1).[110]

In general, therefore, it seems possible, both in theory and in practice, to distinguish the tracing of the guidelines from the actual *ordinatio*,[111] and, in a wider sense, the production and the form of the monument from the text it was intended to exhibit. This is also the case in several milestones, where the panel provided for the inscription, framed and often projecting, was mass-produced and then could not contain all the necessary information, so that part of it had to be cut lower down on the stone.

VI

ERRORS: THEIR CAUSES AND THEIR LESSONS

It was on the basis of the principles that monumental writing follows the evolution of common script and never precedes it, and that, in the sequence of technical phases, the written draft of a text to be engraved is the paramount factor, that Mallon formulated his 'theory of errors'. The results of this approach were remarkable not only for the reading of formulae and of texts, but above all in aiding us to reconstruct on solid and rigorously scientific foundations, the outlines of a history of writing and of culture in general, seen against the whole of their background. In this chapter we shall discuss 'errors' along the lines followed above in speaking of the 'unfinished' texts, and shall briefly touch on a few new points.

Mallon's examples, the 'Pierres fautives' mentioned at the beginning of this work,[112] are indeed very apt; following Mallon,[113] we shall add what can be gleaned from the texts which survive in two editions and to which we have already alluded.[114] Another French scholar, J. Marcillet-Jaubert, in a work as important as those of Mallon himself,[115] has re-established a more critical relationship between epigraphy and the philological disciplines, and has cautioned scholars against eagerly scrutinizing the anomalies of an epigraphic text for secure evidence of popular speech or of local phonetic variations, without first examining the letters themselves from a

D

strictly palaeographical point of view. In the exegesis of a text, it is only reasonable to begin with a proper evaluation of the actual letter in its graphic aspect and of the way in which it came to be where it is, before considering what phonetic value it was meant to have. It would be difficult to disagree with Marcillet-Jaubert when he stresses the new possibility of dating inscriptions by examining errors which perhaps occur with some frequency from a certain period onwards, provided it can be proved that they derive from a confusion already present in the written draft because of the similarity of two letters in common script. (Among the numerous examples mentioned by him, one deserves particular attention: the confusion between *a* and *v* in the common script from the third century A.D.) I am inclined to think that the same error, repeated in different texts of the same period, is evidence—such as we must always look for—of the validity of the palaeographical explanation of the error itself. In isolated cases of error, unfortunately all too numerous, many other factors must be considered, but these factors are often bound up with circumstances which must elude us.

It is very important not to disregard plain inattentiveness as one such factor. We shall never know whether this or that *ordinator* (or rather *scriptor*) or stonecutter—for inattentiveness and casual errors are possible at all stages—was in fact distracted or thinking of other things when he wrote or carved a particular text. We can, however, look around at what happens in our own day: illiteracy is almost eliminated and the means by which the art of writing is diffused ensure that written language and transcription are almost wholly free from regional and local influences; yet we can discover glaring errors in a large number of tablets and inscriptions on stone, even in pretentious ones. I hope the reader will pardon me if I mention by way of example two public monuments placed in prominent positions in their respective cities. At Ceglie Messapico, the Memorial to the Unknown Soldier, in the main square, contains several errors. Some have been corrected, others still remain: STVRORE, probably for STVPORE (there are traces of an attempt at correcting the V), and ASEENDEVA for ASCEN-DEVA; also, an N had been engraved upside down and on it the correct form was later superimposed, the result resembling a figure 8 turned sideways. The other instance is also taken from rather a small city, although there is no lack of such examples in big cities: in Sarsina, the monument to Plautus was inscribed with the word NACQE instead of NACQVE, was unveiled in this state, and was only later corrected by means of an insertion recognizable as such to this day. There-fore, when a Roman cutter engraved E where he should have engraved F for *filius* (as is the case in an inscription now in Vienna),[116] the error may be due to the draft, which was perhaps written in cursive majuscule, that is to say in a script which renders both F and E by two vertical strokes, one slightly longer than the other; but it can easily be due to mere absent-mindedness, especially considering that this abbreviation was thoroughly familiar to both *scriptor* and stonecutter. If, on the other hand, ready-made patterns were sometimes available for the letters, the cutter could, out of negligence or ignorance— or both—have picked up the E instead of the F: we need only remember the possible errors involving movable printing types. This may be the explanation for the LLBERTIS for LIBERTIS in the funerary monument of the Vibii at Tarracina (still unpublished): before this word, and within the space of a few lines in a very short text, the cutter had used the letter L no less than eleven times, and the psychological cause of his error is easy to see. It is equally easy to understand the omission of a letter in this way: an inscription from Rome, now in the Arch-aeological Museum at Perugia,[117] offers a certain instance. It bears the names of two persons, M. RVBBIUS SP. F. and M. RBBIUS M. L.: obviously we are not here in the presence of a second version meant to correct the first. To sum up, Hübner's remarks with regard to the *vitia lapidariorum*[118] are still valid and worthy of attentive consideration. Mallon stresses the importance of errors occurring in common words and everyday expressions; yet precisely in these cases many other factors can intervene to produce the error. The error may even really reflect a linguistic phenomenon. In Ephesus, the western gate of the Hellenistic Agora carries an honorary inscription to Agrippa, with the abbreviation IMB for *imperator*: is this due to a misreading of the written draft, to inattention, or to engraving from dictation, with the error due to local pronunciation? When we say that the draft may have been dictated to the *scriptor*, what do we mean by 'dictated'? Was the copy spelled out letter by letter, or (if need be) abbreviation by abbreviation; or word by word, with the *scriptor* left to decide himself on the suitable abbreviations? In general, I am inclined to believe that, whenever the text was dictated to the *scriptor*, this was done word by word: that might help to explain, among other things, the frequent occurrence of double consonants for single sounds and *vice versa*, where the speaker introduced his local pronunciation and thus corrupted the original.

To sum up: we must envisage a fairly complex relationship, full of uncertainties and misunderstandings, among the different participants in the production of an epigraphic monument,[119] and we must include the possibility that they were the same person. In other words, the 'logical' sequence of phases postulated by Mallon need not be, either always or at all, the 'historical' sequence; not to mention the fact that there is no certainty that the written draft was always, or nearly always, in common minuscule.[120] What were the thoughts of the stonecutter who produced the inscription on the stele of C. Rufellius Rufus at Pola, when he came to the word VIVVS —which in the inscriptions of this and other regions is often spelled VIVS and was perhaps pronounced without sounding the middle V—and simply skipped a space for this letter, leaving it blank?[121] He was prone to errors, it is true, as this same inscription proves. But it is also possible that he simply could not accept this word VIVVS as the *ordinator* must have drawn it for him; or else he failed to see the point of that middle V which appeared in the draft, and he left a blank till he should find somebody to enlighten him; but then, since the meaning remained clear, he let it go at that. Each inscription has its own story and occasionally we can catch a glimpse of it, although quite often it must remain wholly hidden from us.

Corrections of carved texts, as well as additions to them, made in antiquity either in the process of production or shortly after, are, in my opinion, a factor of major importance in the exegesis of inscriptions. Omitted letters inserted later in smaller characters; the crowding of two letters into the space previously occupied by one (such as ERNIS later corrected in this way to ERONIS in the inscription of L. Tonneius L. l. Ero at Ephesus); the replacement of an incorrect letter—all these show to what extent either the workmen themselves, right in the shop, or their customers, or public opinion, were alert to error. They give us a clue to the educational standards of the times[122]— even though we cannot altogether exclude the possibility that, where the error seems to us to have remained uncorrected, a correction was in fact painted in, as Oliver has recently pointed out.[123]

So far a great deal of attention has been paid to deliberate erasures on public monuments, since they are connected with political events of major importance, such as *damnatio memoriae*.[124] For different reasons the same attention must now be paid to corrections present on any text whatsoever. As for additions, they above all can reveal to us the historical development of sensitivity in selecting what was considered worthy of being committed to stone. Of particular interest are the additions between the lines or on the margins and borders. At times these additions are mere onomastic notations, as is the case in a Roman inscription now in Trevi,[125] where the *nomen gentilicium* has been added above the *cognomen*; if, however, it is the *cognomen* or the *agnomen* that has been added, then we are in the presence of a very interesting phase in onomastic development.[126] In this respect, the well-known *elogium* of C. Castricius Calvus, called Agricola, at Forlí, with some most interesting expressions added between the lines, may be considered a prime example of a text which transcends its particular significance to reveal unsuspected psychological and social factors, still in process of development.[127] Sometimes, again, the insertion or addition merely represents the remedy for what was forgotten by either the customer, or the *scriptor*, or the *ordinator*, or the stonecutter, in the same way as for any simple carving error.[128]

A question arises: in the complex play of contributions to the finished epigraphic product, is it possible to single out any element which can be ascribed to the influence of the written draft more readily than to any other factor, just as it has been possible to conclude that the preparation of the surface in the stonemason's shop also included the tracing of the guidelines? I am not convinced that the structure of the text—e.g. 'paragraphed' or 'centered', in the words used by the Gordons,[129] according to whether the first letter of a 'thought unit' protruded beyond the left margin or was indented—was usually specified in the draft; nor that the written draft already indicated interpuncts, apices, supralineates (I should say it could more easily show *sigla* and abbreviations), or that it roughly indicated the module of the letters, or that it called for different modules in the same inscription. On the other hand, I believe that the draft is responsible for those instances of arrangement which appear to take no account of the shape of the panel provided for the text or of the structure of the monument. For example: almost everywhere in Italy, sepulchral stelae are to be found (especially from the Republican period), which show a door on the front. Usually in these monuments the inscription is engraved on the lintel, or, if two persons are involved, each uses one of the door-leaves for his name. (This is true also for the front of many small urns of the second century A.D.) Yet there are cases, as on a small stele (still unpublished) in the National Museum at Chieti, in which the inscription runs across from one leaf to the other, climbing across the central listels: in this case the artisan has perhaps too passively followed the pattern of the written draft. This fact is still more evident when inscriptions referring to two different persons are placed one next to the other on the front of the same monument, without any architectural or decorative element separating the two, so that they run together as if they were one text; as is the case (for instance) in a stele in the British Museum.[130] We are here in the presence of the most complete indifference on the part of either *ordinator* or stonecutter towards the logical arrangement of the text; in this case the artisan has indeed followed the two drafts letter by letter without even 'seeing' what was produced by his hands. As Daux has recently observed,[131] this attitude is also that of the artisan who engraved his text on a stone at Stratoni which already contained another engraved inscription, so that the two texts blend together line by line and mislead the reader by the apparent plausibility of the blend.

It was the *ordinator*, or perhaps even the stonecutter, who (I believe) usually saw to the arrangement of the text, taking into account the shape of the monument, as did the man who produced the Republican inscription of C. Torbanius L. f. at Fano:[132] he carried the final S of the *nomen* over to the second line, not because of any lack of space in the first line, but out of sheer love of symmetry; and this cannot be ascribed to the person composing the written draft, but only to one intimately familiar with monuments. Similarly, the artisan in charge of the inscription of the Tatii at Tarracina[133] preferred to write the names and the titles each on its own separate line and arranged a double alignment with the beginnings of lines in precise alternation.

To sum up: the whole arrangement of the text was probably the responsibility of the workshop, and this included the decision whether to have a straight left margin in perfect alignment or whether to lay out the text with an eye to symmetry—and sometimes with due regard for certain 'thought units', which have a line to themselves[134]—although quite often the central axis is displaced slightly to the left. But though the arrangement of the text was the responsibility of the shop, the fact that towards the right margin the letters are often crowded, or else grow smaller, or even protrude beyond it, leads me to believe that the *ordinatio* of the letters was often a very rough one, as indeed the Gordons have remarked on more than one occasion. I think, in fact, that where it involved a full preliminary tracing, the result is a better distribution of the letters; but that where we have an excessively irregular layout, there was no preparatory tracing (for if this had been done in charcoal or chalk, it could have been perfectly corrected without fear of leaving unsightly marks on the stone), and reliance on the stonecutter's eye was all there was by way of *ordinatio*. I would go so far as to believe that quite often the customer only supplied the personal data concerning the one to be commemorated on the stone,[135] and that it was the responsibility of the workshop to cast these data in the language proper to inscriptions, to add certain formulae, and (inevitably according to the fashion of place and time) to choose either the nominative or the genitive or the dative for the name that came after the *adprecatio* to the *Dei Manes*.

Moreover, I believe that the choice of abbreviations (whether by suspension or by contraction) was often left to the shop and not stated in the draft, except, of course, in the case of public texts important enough to require from the writer the competent use of *sigla* more familiar to diplomatic practice than to stonemasons' workshops. In addition, the shop was undoubtedly responsible for the drafting of texts somehow derived from one main text, such as dedicatory inscriptions on a number of bases forming part of a single votive monument,[136] or the cippi along the sides of a sepulchral *area*, where the name of the dedicator or of the deceased is often reduced to a few *siglae*. The shops, of course, were familiar with the most common abbreviations, and their practical experience complemented those manuals which were apparently in wide use, if indeed we believe that the C. Titius Probus who, it seems, compiled the list of *praenomina* later epitomized and transmitted with the text of Valerius Maximus also compiled a manual of epigraphic abbreviations. On the other hand, the workshops would rely entirely on the draft for graphic elements that were utterly new and unfamiliar to them. For example, we have a Republican inscription from Teramo[137] where the names of the *duoviri* occupy the first two lines and mention of their office is made to the right of these lines, on a separate line placed halfway between the other two; to avoid any misunderstanding as to the attribution of this magistracy to both names, the cutter incised a crotchet next to each name as if to bracket the two lines bearing the names. This was obviously present in the draft submitted to him and the cutter faithfully copied it.

Finally, I think that, besides *sigla* and abbreviations, the workshop quite freely used existing manuals, suggested their use to the customers, and employed their expressions in the texts. I am not convinced by Mallon when he considers the closing formula '*ici reposent*' of a draft from a modern workshop in Algiers on the same level as the rest of the text.[138] The use of an expression of this kind may be due to custom, while the work of the cutter in carving it is influenced by familiarity with an expression he has used hundreds of times. Accordingly, the draft here plays no significant role, whether it was composed within or outside the shop, and a cutter's error can hardly be due to anything other than mere oversight. This consideration weakens Mallon's own theory in so far as he attaches the greatest importance to errors occurring in common expressions. Before him, in an article constantly ignored but still valid,[139] Cagnat had already outlined the features of manuals and of collections for trade purposes, with their formulae, verses and epigrams, as they were available to workshops, thus providing a background and relationships that had no necessary connection with the general history of writing as such or even with the history of the language. In the immense community of the Roman Empire, these manuals constitute a framework of which Cagnat has indeed distinguished the outlines, without, however, supplying it wherever possible with its individual content: the network of stonemasons' shops. It is obvious that study of set phrases, proverbs, philosophical maxims used in different and perhaps in widely distant places, opens a window on the contribution of these workshops to the formation of a common physiognomy of Roman culture, besides revealing otherwise unknown and unsuspected aspects of the psychology of those individuals who chose or accepted the expressions concerned.

In conclusion we may say that *sigla* and ligatures (especially the latter, as they are characteristic of lapidary techniques and answer a need for economy which is proper to writing on stone much more than to writing on papyrus)—these as well as formulae, phrases, stereotyped expressions, the features of the monument, the choice of symbols and of decorative elements, the preparation of the surface for the inscription, the tracing of the guidelines and the carving of the text—all these elements, with the addition of palaeographic or linguistic phenomena (especially archaisms), combine to provide an epigraphic environment embodied in one or more workshops. Just as in palaeography there are the 'scriptorial provinces' with their *sciptoria*, so for epigraphy we can formulate the concept of an epigraphic environment and its stonemasons' workshops.

Research in this direction is more profitable in peripheral regions, where these phenomena arrive more slowly and endure more tenaciously. This is shown by the excellent work of Spanish epigraphists[140] and can be gathered from epigraphic publications concerning peripheral Roman provinces.[141] I have been able to observe this even in Italy: in the Salentine peninsula, in the farthest recess of the heel of Italy;[142] at Ravenna, where the presence of the fleet created a sharply defined human *milieu*;[143] and finally at Urbino, where epigraphic production absorbed the cultural heritage of a unique enclave, that of the Galli Senones.[144]

VII

THE INSCRIPTION AS A CULTURAL MONUMENT

The phases which Mallon considers essential in the production of an inscription—the 'logical' phases, one might say—are the written draft, the *ordinatio*, and finally the carving. All these must be defined very carefully, because at each level, for each phase, three fundamental factors intervene: first, the availability of, or the tendency to use, particular formulae or particular abbreviations and stereotyped expressions; secondly, the precise—or confused—requirements of the customer who is actually the prime mover in the evolution of epigraphic semantics (though we must add that this evolution may also be promoted by the originality or education of a particular work-man); and lastly, the level of education of all the participants in this long 'production line', to any one of whom an error (and Mallon rightly stresses its importance for the knowledge of palaeography) may be due, at every level and at every stage. Naturally, it is most likely that an error is due to the *ordinator* or *scriptor*; but it is equally possible that, in the case of cheaper products, *scriptor* and *sculptor* are one person, or that one corrects the other. At any rate, it would be necessary to know, in each case, what was the range of these men's education, what instrumental or mnemonic equipment they had accumulated from their respective experience, and to be able to recapture the genesis of any given inscription, as well as to isolate the psychological matrix of each phenomenon, in an historical process which often eludes us. It would also be necessary to know the *milieu*, defined in the widest sense, within which both the artisans and their patrons moved, and to bear in mind the official scribes and the village scribes, the men of letters who wrote verses, the lapidary and epigraphic schools which must have existed in some centres, before we reach the illustrious examples of Filocalus and the inscriptions of Damasus. 'On a difficilement idée de la place qu'a tenue le marbrier, le lapicide, dans la civilisation classique', says Louis Robert in a paper now fundamental for the understanding of classical epigraphy,[145] as he recalls the amazement of the traveller who sees in Roman Africa, in Syria or Anatolia, an immense wealth of still extant inscriptions; and, in the case of a European territory, he remarks how accurately one can gauge its Romanization by the presence, the density and the character of the extant epigraphic material. This means that the stonecutter's trade was important and widely diffused; accordingly there must have been teachers and schools where it could be learnt, even if this meant only apprenticeship in one of the larger workshops. Now, precisely because lapidary writing and epigraphic idiom were the object of conscious research and study, we must believe all the more in the possibility of tracing the outlines of a history of epigraphic monuments, so as to reach, shop by shop, dating criteria that can offer some elements of reliability and can overcome the scepticism traditional among epigraphists.[146] It is difficult to agree *tout court* with Thylander when he remarks that the craftsmen who worked on public monuments tried more than any others to follow the changes imposed by palaeography,[147] for in fact the conservatism of shops which produced official monuments according to models linked to classicist and archaizing conventions is well known. Perhaps we should first solve the problem of 'educated' art; we shall never know to what extent this type of art in the Roman provinces is the work of

local artisans and how much of it is due to specialists imported
from elsewhere and not directly connected with the local shops.
Still, research studies like those of Anna Sadurska on ornamental motifs,[148] or attempts—like the exemplary one of Audin
and Burnand—to classify chronologically the epigraphic output
of a large Roman centre, are worthy of serious consideration.[149]

Reflection on the wider context within which any epigraphic
monument must be assessed will inevitably lead us to seek to
understand the role which inscriptions played in the cultural
shaping of men. In a well-known passage of the *Satyricon*,
Hermeros boasts: 'lapidarias litteras scio'.[150] The expression
is vague: it must mean that Hermeros can at any rate read large
block capitals, but not necessarily that he can write them.[151]
Again, it may be intended to be witty or pompous. On the
other hand, inscriptions were a permanent element of the daily
visual environment of the citizen (and I mean, above all, the
city dweller—it applies much less to people in the country).
Hence it is fair to assume that they could not fail to exercise
an educational influence; honorary and votive inscriptions,
inscriptions on the pediments of buildings and especially on
sepulchral stelae, probably constituted the best reading practice,
intentional or otherwise, for many adults and children alike.
Moreover, it was through inscriptions more than through any
other medium that political concepts were propagated and the
historical memories of country and family perpetuated. From
the moment he left the *pomerium* and started out towards the
country, the traveller passing through the necropolis of a
Roman city would relive its true history: the only history
which, after the death of its eyewitnesses, could and indeed had
to stay alive in men's memories. In analysing some texts of
major interest, epigraphists often forget to take into account
the echoes which politicians planned that these texts should
evoke, and above all the lasting—the almost eternal—heritage
which, by helping to create traditions, they would leave for the

imagination and culture of posterity. I have attempted to provide some evidence for this by an analysis of an inscription in honour of C. Marius in the Forum at Ariminum.[152] Certain expressions—for instance, certain acclamations and imperial titles—are bestowed, among other reasons, with a view to the psychological impression they are intended to produce. This concept is quite familiar to archaeologists, for they know that official marble portraiture gives an idealized, propagandist image of the ruler. This has remained unchanged right down to modern times, to some extent surviving even the invention of photography and lasting at least until the introduction of films and television. What mattered most was the head, often replaced on the same statue, as is still the case in many churches (in some it is even established practice) where, at the accession of a new pope, only the head is changed in the pope's portrait. Formulae and titles serve much the same purpose as, for instance, clothes or hair-styles; they are immediately recognized and imitated by the public, as is well known to the modern experts who conduct market research before launching a new cosmetic product, or a new actress, or the latest rock-and-roll singer.

The importance of lapidary writing in the Classical world cannot, however, be fully appreciated, if we fail to consider that in many a culture it represented a novelty, something that had grown amidst difficulties over a number of centuries. We do not know to what extent some populations used pictograms in the first stages of their development, nor to what extent in historical times they remembered the existence of these pictograms; and, if so, whether they were aware of the stages through which their writing, by then phonetic, had had to pass (at least in some areas) in moving from a syllabic to an alphabetical structure, with the indispensable contribution of more advanced cultures, whether near at hand or far away. But writing, which in an entirely conventional manner rendered

ritual formulae, prayers and ceremonial prescriptions, as it does
in the most ancient epigraphic documents, must certainly have
first appeared as a magical instrument, largely beyond compre-
hension. Thus writing came to be used for communicating
with the deity, as for example in the inscribed nails which were
traditionally driven into the walls of temples. The magical
properties often ascribed to alphabet tables are well known, and
to a large extent cryptographic and symbolic writing, so highly
in favour with some pagan sects and with the Christian religion,
have their distant origin in this primitive ritual respect for
alphabetical symbols. We must also remember that in many
parts of the ancient world writing on stone was introduced, or
rather was spread, by the Romans, so that it came to appear as a
characteristic instrument of the master race. Perhaps we must
invoke this fact, in addition to the ritual fear felt towards
writing as a magical and incomprehensible phenomenon, to
explain the insult often scribbled on Italian walls against
'whoever reads this'; to understand the practical joke played on
the person who takes the trouble to read the graffito, only to
discover that he is 'an ass'.

The concrete relationship, living and ever new, which links
an inscription to its reader, must also be examined with regard
to the standpoint from which the reader must view the text in
order to understand it without effort. There are contrivances
and sensations familiar to the modern man which must have
been wholly unknown in Classical antiquity. We do not know
whether it was customary then, as it is now, to hang name-
plates, or signs marking shops or public offices, on a support
projecting from the wall, so that they would appear in frontal
perspective to a pedestrian walking along the street; in any case,
these would hardly have been stone signs, but almost always
perishable *tabulae dealbatae*. It is certain, however, that vertical
inscriptions—i.e. inscriptions to be read from the top down—
not to mention inscriptions containing upside-down lettering,

were not in use, as they are today. The only exceptions were some Greek *horoi* of various types and some sacred or sepulchral cippi, also in Greek.[153] In fact, today we read signs as we walk, without stopping, along the pavement, whereas in antiquity, in order to read an inscription, or indeed any written notice, one had to stop, as one does today only to look at a poster or a window-display. The only exceptions in antiquity were milestones: a traveller, provided he was going in the direction of the writing, could grasp the general sense as well as the details of the text without stopping his carriage or his horse—a manœuvre more difficult than it is today to slow down or to stop one's car to read a traffic sign. It must be remembered that we should find it difficult to read our road signs quickly if they were set on a curved surface, like inscriptions on milestones.[154] The modern world has also worked revolutionary changes in plates, road signs and advertisement through the use of artificial light, which at night enlivens the skyline of our cities,[155] and through the use of 'moving inscriptions', either flashing intermittently on stationary signs, or carried on moving vehicles, such as advertisements displayed on the sides of large lorries or buses.

The fundamental principle of a Roman inscription in relation to the passer-by along the street or road is, therefore, that it faces him only when he stops and turns to look at it. The Romans were builders of roads as well as great travellers, and the *siste viator et lege* which, in various forms, is to be seen on so many inscriptions must be considered in the context of this human reality: a brief pause, the perusal of a *titulus* on a *monimentum*, and another thread is woven in the fabric of a culture based on tradition and politics—the culture of a people that travels far from home, opens up forests, paves roads and measures all distances from Rome. This is why the column-shaped little cippi with their slender necks, so common in Greece in the burial grounds of slaves and humble folk, took

E

on a more flattened shape, till they came to resemble a stele with a rounded top and the front entirely covered by the inscription. We can see the transitional stage of this development in certain Salentine cippi in the shape of truncated cones, with an inscribed panel projecting from the shaft.[156] Again, the Greek and Hellenistic stelae bearing in relief the representation of lively scenes full of movement and three-dimensional effects were replaced for Roman taste by tall boxes, from which the portraits of the dead, shoulder to shoulder, gaze frontally at the passer-by. For the Roman stonemason, the only one to be taken into account is the passer-by who stops to read along the way, but does not come closer or bend down to read excessively small characters, such as one sees in the inscriptions of so many Greek *agorai* and Greek temples. Nor does the Roman envisage a solitary converse with the heavens, as in some oriental inscriptions. What he strives for is the practical possibility of being read and understood by all: large letters, and the more distant the larger, even when the contents of the text would rather call for uniformity of lettering.[157] The rule of frontality remains unbroken even where the inscription is on the drum of a cylindrical monument, such as the tomb of Caecilia Metella, through the device of engraving it on a framed inset. There are few exceptions to that rule: the surveyors' cippi, like those from the Gracchan period, derived, as has been recently shown, from Etruscan originals like those found at Marzabotto not long ago;[158] milestones;[159] inscriptions on *mensae ponderariae*; dedications on the rims of sacred basins, as on the *labra* of the Bona Dea; some signatures on the bases of statues; and, of course, mosaic inscriptions, and indeed all inscriptions on floors. But there is no parallel among the Romans for some practices of the Greek world: e.g. votive inscriptions such as those placed on the horizontal top of a pedestal supporting a sculptured pair of feet dedicated *pro reditu*, as in the temple of Aesculapius in Epidaurus and elsewhere; or the sepulchral disks of Kasos, which, as recent excavations have shown, were used to close small tumuli and were placed on the surface of the ground directly above the head of the person buried, so that a face becomes a name to be remembered by posterity.[160] One further anomaly is represented in the Roman world by some sepulchral cippi from Vaison in Provence, of the familiar disk shape also seen in the Roman cippi of Adria, bearing on the front the name of the deceased and on the back—for once used for an inscription— the measurements of the burial plot. Finally, as an example of concern for the reader's point of view, we have inscriptions engraved backwards, to be read from a point of view opposite to that of the engraver, as in numerous glass cups, in which the legend was meant to be read by the user in the act of drinking— that is to say, from the inside of the cup. We have an analogous situation in the case of funerary inscriptions (especially Christian), where a sacred name is so cut as to be read (notionally) by the deceased and not by the onlooker.

In many ways this discussion places the problem of the relationship between the inscription—or rather, the inscribed surface—and the monument in which it is set in a new light. This relationship must always be carefully assessed, because it leads to observations valuable in several respects. In this connection, Attilio Degrassi's work on the original location of the consular and triumphal *Fasti*, by its use of all available data, is a model of rigorous method.[161] The relation between inscription and monument has been differently assessed by different scholars. Klaffenbach, for example, gives a substantially negative verdict,[162] for he denies any complementary relationship between the two; he considers the inscription as something tacked on to the monument, something used to date and explain the monument, except that he allows some ornamental value to inscriptions of the imperial period. My own (very different) opinions have been expressed on several occasions,[163] and those observations and ideas have been accepted by Mansuelli.[164] Finally, Rehm has drawn attention to the artistic correlation that can exist between the inscription and its monument, especially when the latter presents structural and decorative elements of some interest.[165] Actually, the epigraphist is not concerned with stylistic canons; he merely seeks to capture a glimpse of the cultural background and the framework of ideas, through which a text came to be considered suitable for, or necessarily linked with, a particular monumental design. This remains true even when the inscription, usually very brief, is on a small panel incised or painted in a marginal area of the monument: the artist's signature; or, in mosaics, the names of persons and beasts represented; or the names of deities on the chest of large statues in the Roman provinces, essential if these deities were to be identified by a public still unfamiliar with Roman ways. There are times when the inscription seems to be swallowed up by the monumental complex. Occasionally, again, the inscribed panel itself shows a miniature representation of a substantial monument, which in turn bears an inscription with the names of the deceased.[166] Again, there are instances, though they are rare, of inscriptions engraved on little bronze plaques later affixed to small urns or other objects: in this case, the complete product is probably due to two different workshops, and the combination of monument and inscription may be the result of a choice made outside the general environment of the workshops, to which we have constantly been referring. The same conclusion can be drawn for those extremely rare monuments which were made up by the addition of a portrait bust, separately produced and sometimes of a different material, to a cippus or stele bearing the inscription.[167]

VIII

CONCLUSION: EPIGRAPHY AND HISTORY

When speaking of inscriptions and monuments, we are inevitably led to discuss the problem of the alleged relationship between two disciplines, epigraphy and archaeology. This is not, as might appear, idle chatter: a large part of Mallon's work —and of other scholars' as well—is based on the relationship between epigraphy and another important discipline, palaeography. Moreover, we must remember that epigraphy has often been defined as the science which 'prepares' material for the archaeologist and the historian. This definition is in fact merely the last modest legacy of academic and scholarly ways of thought that held sway down to the nineteenth century, down to Furtwängler and Mommsen (though one should mention, among earlier scholars, Winckelmann, and even some views of G. B. Vico: that is to say, down to the time when the old and glorious *Antiquitates*, the courses in epigraphy and numismatics, were ousted by history of art and political history. Both these disciplines then acquired autonomous status, as subjects for learned enquiry and for teaching, whereas epigraphy was relegated to the rank of an 'ancillary' discipline, often and openly the object of scorn (even on the part of Mommsen, who yet was a prince among epigraphists) whenever the epigraphic datum did not yield a 'useful' conclusion.

It is obvious that, if by archaeology we mean the history of the art or of the artistic concepts of Classical antiquity, epigraphy stands in the same relation of mutual benefit to it as to any other discipline. If, on the other hand, we consider archaeology a method of understanding and describing the origin and history of a phenomenon in the light of its surviving evidence, then, to use a recent and felicitous expression, the title of this present study could well be 'The Archaeology of Epigraphy'. It is once more Mallon who stresses[168] the existence of an archaeology of 'inscribed' monuments: that is to say, of any object (of any epoch) bearing some writing, like papyri, inscriptions, *instrumenta*, codices, etc. This discipline is not concerned with writing as such ('l'écriture étant impalpable entre le support et l'agent d'exécution'), but with 'l'homme écrivant' —man as a writer, in all his aspects, such as, for example, his position in the act of writing, his way of holding his writing implement, the angle between the latter and the line of writing, and furthermore, *ordinatio* and similar matters. All this is well known to palaeographers, as is shown by the exceedingly important observations made by Cencetti on the manner in which the Forum cippus, the most ancient document in Latin,[169] was engraved. Proceeding along this road, we end, with Mallon, by criticizing the traditional definition of epigraphy according to the material used ('un critère obscur de la science officielle: celui des monuments durables'),[170] and considering a single distinction as of critical use: that between documents produced in one operation, with intermediate stages, and documents produced by a process involving several stages, like most inscriptions on stone.

Silvio Ferri takes us further. He stresses the need for an 'archaeological' examination of the inscription,[171] for a total assessment of all that accompanies the text on the monument (Mallon already complained that the text often tends to eclipse the monument):[172] all this must be seen as inseparable from the inscription, that is to say, from that complex of technical and traditional factors which leads to the act of carving it. At this point we are not far from Robert's position, when he stresses the bond between the inscription and the world that saw its birth, or, as I would rather say, that gave it birth.[173]

In fact, his 'dedicatory inscription to the nymphs', even if found, could well be something left behind by a casual traveller or by a madman or by a hermit—in other words, it could be something without any apparent link with the social background in which we should wish to place it. Yet, it would still be the mark of a particular culture, of a civilization, which by means of this inscription left a message that it meant to endure. What I really mean is that inscriptions help us reconstruct, not the history of the individual as it actually was—as we might do if we could hear a taped conversation of his or read his letters— but the individual as he wanted to appear vis-à-vis both contemporary and future society: his interlocutor is impersonal and general—a whole culture, whose specific epigraphy we must and can study. Once again Robert supports us by observing that there is no one science of epigraphy valid for all cultures and all societies.[174] As I have pointed out on other occasions, the Greek carves the *acta* of his *polis* or of his religion, while the Roman, on the whole, prefers to state the individual's relationship to his deity or (through the *cursus honorum*) to his own political society; but most of all he wants to insert the individual chronologically in the cycle of the generations of his family. For the only chronology the Roman knows is that which links him, in the eyes of posterity, to a father or to a patron, and ultimately, at several removes, to the founder of the clan. The Roman inscription, and the funerary inscription in particular, completely ignores any other chronological indication: it is a history of individuals, a historiography of *nomina*, of common people, still alive after death in the act of prayer, in their membership of a *gens*, in the service they gave to the *res publica*. There is a whole history to be written here, to be put together by means of inscriptions: history of men—of societies and cultures in their various stages—who chose to be remembered for the future through a monument that transmits their names, their features, or both; or the record or symbols of their trades, their public offices and their religious dignities; sometimes with the man's name and portrait (sometimes even a full-size statue), but sometimes entirely on their own; next a history of the workshops, of the whole epigraphic background; and finally a history of what men thought and felt when they ensured their survival into a future society, in a world to which survival was important. Thus, even from a philosophical point of view, the 'civilisation de l'épigraphie'[175] of the Classical world can be clearly outlined and distinguished from that of the ancient East and even more from that of the modern world. Robert was right to observe that we cannot consider as real epigraphic documents of our own day the various instruments of our economic life, such as plaques, shop-signs or advertising posters,[176] mostly made of material as easily transformed and re-used as that of the *alba* of Classical antiquity.[177] In our age, he thinks, the only inscriptions that seem analogous to those of the ancient world are those on honorary pedestals or on public monuments, such as dedicatory and commemorative inscriptions—and these are themselves inspired by, or (as in the case of religious inscriptions) are the direct continuation of, the practice of the Classical world. In fact, we often forget that for centuries now ours has been a civilization of printed paper. Let us bear the consequences of this in mind; let us consider the fact that whereas the inscription is a public document—open, unconcealed, seen by all—the printed page is folded up, and it is put away on the shelf as easily as it is difficult to displace a heavy inscription. To read an inscription we must move, we must go to the place where it is located; while the printed page travels and reaches all, or at least a great many, of us; it carries a message, the same message, to any number of very different people; it creates bonds among them, makes them—one might almost say—into accomplices or proselytes, and thus, to a large extent, it reaches beyond the limits of its original environment, cultural and social, which was all that the message of a Greek or Roman inscription could reach, even as the faintest echo. Consequently, inscriptions no longer perform in the modern world the function they performed in antiquity; and so the image of a Roman road lined on both sides by stelae and epigraphic monuments—so dear to artists from the Renaissance onwards, so different from our cemeteries, removed as they are from the main highways, shut away behind high walls and bristling with headstones—that image is replaced for us by the visual horizon of Fifth Avenue, as we are used to seeing it on film or television, in daytime or even more at night: the moving, multi-coloured lights of the traffic travelling through a dark furrow fenced on both sides by high walls of brightly flashing neon lights, which represent the beckoning of what is at that moment static, fixed in an ephemeral immobility—factories, shops, theatres—to what is going past: to pedestrians, motorists, and other vehicles—in fact, to humanity in rapid motion.

A final reflection: we have already agreed with Mallon that the criterion of durable material is not entirely valid in defining epigraphy as a science. On the other hand, it is also a fact that Mallon speaks as a palaeographer and, as I pointed out at the beginning, does not bother to investigate whether epigraphy is a separate discipline from palaeography or whether it has lost its dignity as an independent science. Yet Mallon also stresses the importance of judging a document by the intentions of the person who wrote it,[178] and these intentions may be independent of the material on which the text is written: a papyrus can clearly contain a private letter or an imperial rescript, and a stone can bear a scratched note or a funerary inscription. But the 'intention' of which Mallon speaks does depend on the nature of the text, and above all on its destination. At this point we can add our own definition: epigraphy is the historical study of the manner in which certain ideas were chosen to be displayed for public and permanent information; or, to put it the Roman way, to become *monimenta*. In fact, the purpose of inscriptions—as a great epigraphist, Hiller von Gärtringen, has remarked—is well defined by Greek cities in the concluding formula of their public decrees: 'This decree shall be engraved on a stone stele and set up in the sanctuary.'[179]

This definition establishes the inscription as the act of an individual who reflects on his death, and trusts in something after it, to assume concrete and palpable form; for in fact the person who entrusts his message to a tombstone inscription is addressing a future society, which he envisages as valuing this message and before which he wants to assert himself. In the Classical world it is indeed a much rarer occurrence—and accordingly a very precious datum in a quest to trace the history of ideas—to find the inscription addressing a god, or the underworld; for example, it is probably in the underworld that the gold *laminae* containing the instructions for the last journey were meant to be useful to the initiates in the Orphic mysteries, or the open rolls with the account of their earthly life to the Etruscans, amidst the cheerless revelry of a Lasa, a Charun or an Orcus. Such use in another world was also intended for the equipment that adorned the burials of Greeks and Romans; yet this equipment was hidden in the tomb and was in no way meant to distinguish them in the eyes of either their survivors or future society.[180] We have, after all, no other way of knowing the men and the cultures of the Classical world except the one they themselves chose for ensuring their survival—the way which, in the widest sense, we may call that of epigraphy. Once again, then, history unfolds as the conscious historiography of individuals, whom we can come to know only because they took the trouble of establishing a dialogue with their own society. The only alternative to this perspective is a way that seems unnatural, improper, one might say irreverent: it is to take the measurements of men from the imprints they left in the lava of Vesuvius, or to weigh the ashes and the bones on the vast accursed fields of Trasimene and Cannae.

NOTES

1 *MH* X (1953), pp. 141–160.
2 *Libyca* II (1954), pp. 187–199; III (1955), pp. 307–327 and 435–459.
3 Mallon, *op. cit.* (note 1). Among Mallon's other contributions the following should be mentioned: 'Scriptoria épigraphiques', *Scriptorium* XI (1957), pp. 177–194; see also *Emerita* XVI (1948), pp. 14–15; *Libyca* III (1955), pp. 155–162; *ibid.* VII (1959), pp. 111–120 (see J. Lassus, in *Atti del terzo Congr. intern. di Epigrafia*, Roma 1959, pp. 225–227); 'L'ordinatio des inscriptions', *CRAI* 1955, pp. 126–136.
4 Madrid 1952, pp. 55–73.
5 *Exempla script. epigr. Lat.*, Berlin 1885, *Prolegomena*, pp. 13–84, especially 13–15. (Since all my references to Hübner's work are to the *Prolegomena*, the pages will be more conveniently indicated in Arabic than in Roman numerals.)
6 S.v. 'Inscriptiones', in Daremberg-Saglio, *Dictionnaire des Antiquités*; 'Epigraphie', in *La Grande Encyclopédie*, XVI, Paris 1894, pp. 68 ff.; nothing, on the other hand, is to be found either in Cagnat's famous *Cours* or in other, quite recent, works on Roman epigraphy (e.g. R. Bloch, *L'épigraphie latine*, Paris 1952, reprinted 1964; H. Thylander, *Étude sur l'épigraphie latine*, Lund 1952), with the sole exception of I. Calabi's work, *L'uso storiografico delle iscrizioni latine*, Milano 1953, pp. 15–20. Concerning the subject in general, mention should also be made of H. Leclercq's contribution, 'Inscriptions latines chrétiennes', in *Dictionnaire d'Archéologie chrétienne et de*

Liturgie (1925), coll. 716–728, especially for the development of new epigraphic monuments in the early Christian period, for the analysis of 'errors' and of interpolations in inscribed texts, as well as for texts only partially carved and with the rest legible in the graffito incision of the *ordinator*. See also the interesting survey of epigraphic studies by G. Bagnani, in *Phoenix* XIII (1959), pp. 13–17, and finally, by Mallon himself, the long history of opposition on the part of epigraphists during the last hundred years to a full understanding of the genesis of 'errors' ('L'archéologie des monuments graphiques', *RH* CCXXVI (1961), pp. 297–312 and especially pp. 305 ff.).

7 *Libyca* III (1955), pp. 160–162.

8 *MH*, cited note 1.

9 *Scriptorium* (cited note 3), p. 181, note 6. Let me here state once and for all that, like other scholars, I use the term *ordinator* not because I believe that this term is to be found with this meaning in the ancient sources, but merely to indicate the person who performed the action expressed by the verb *ordinare*.

10 *El concepto de la epigrafía. Consideraciones sobre la necesidad de su ampliación*, Madrid 1953 (see also M. Almagro's review in *Ampurias* XIV (1952, publ. 1953), pp. 292–293). Among the many useful studies by Navascués himself, see also *La dedicación de San Juan de Baños*, Palencia 1961, particularly interesting in that analogous methods are there applied to texts which belong to a later, post-classical, period. Finally, and also for the study of monumental types, see 'Caracteres externos de las antiguas inscripciones salmantinas. Los epitafios de la zona occidental', *Boletín de la Academía de la Historia* CLII (1963), pp. 159–224.

11 *Atti terzo Congr.* (cited note 3), pp. 328–337; *Officine epigrafiche e ceti sociali*, Urbania 1962.

12 *Actes du IIe Congrès intern. d'Épigraphie*, Paris 1953, p. 8; see also A. E. Raubitschek, 'Die Inschrift als geschichtliches Denkmal', *Gymnasium* LXXII (1965), pp. 511–522.

13 'Épigraphie et paléographie', *CRAI* 1955, pp. 195–222, and *ibid.*, pp. 136–137, as a direct reply to Mallon; see also Ch. Samaran's comment, *ibid.*, pp. 220–222, and finally Mallon's

answer, in *Scriptorium* (cited note 3), pp. 180–181, note 5.

14 Robert, *REG* LXXVII (1964), pp. 130–131; Pritchett, *BCH* LXXXVII (1963), p. 20, note 3.

15 *Aegyptus* XXXVII (1957), pp. 295–296; cf. 'La papirologia e l'epigrafia', in *Introduzione alla filologia classica*, Milano 1951, pp. 133–216, and especially pp. 206–209; *Atti terzo Congr.* (cited note 3), pp. 291–298.

16 *RAL* s. 8, XVIII (1963), pp. 195–198, with earlier bibliography.

17 *Album of Dated Latin Inscriptions*, I–IV, Univ. of California Press 1958–1965.

18 Univ. of California Press 1957.

19 Among the numerous reviews of the Gordons' work, see A. Ferrua, *RBPh* XXXVII (1959), pp. 775–777, especially for the technical aspects of the carving; we shall return to this later.

20 *Scriptorium* (cited note 3), p. 179, note 3.

21 *CIL* X, 7296 = *IG* XIV, 297; see Mallon, *MH* (cited note 1), p. 146. A drawing of this inscription is to be found in Hübner, *op. cit.* (note 5), p. 30.

22 *IG, loc. cit.*

23 *Scriptorium* (cited note 3), p. 177, note 1.

24 *Op. cit.* (note 19).

25 *Loc. cit.* (note 23).

26 *CIL* VIII, 2482; E. Albertini and P. Massiéra, *REA* XLI (1939), pp. 234–235 = *L'Année épigraphique*, 1940, nos. 147 and 153.

27 'Scriptor titulorum', in *Enciclopedia dell' Arte antica* VII; see also the still useful survey by E. LeBlant, 'Sur les graveurs des inscriptions antiques', *Revue de l'art chrétien*, 1859, pp. 12–38.

28 *Op. cit.* (note 5), pp. 29–30 and 35–36, with full discussion on the meaning to be ascribed to each of these verbs (similarly in Marquardt, *Das Privatleben der Römer*, Leipzig 1886, p. 625, note 5), and especially on the identification of the action expressed by the verb *sculpere* (*scalpere*). See also Leclercq, 'Lapicides', in *Dict. Arch. chrét. Lit.* (cited note 6), coll. 1326–1328; H. Blümner, *Terminologie der Gewerbe u. Künste bei Griechen u. Römern*, III, Leipzig 1884, p. 7. On the epi-

graphic usage of *scribere* for *scribendum curare*, see A. Degrassi, in *BCAR* LXXVIII (1961–1962, publ. 1964), p. 142, where this same quotation from Propertius (IV, 7, 83–86) is also to be found.

29 *CIL* X, 6193 (Formiae).

30 *CIL* VI, 9557 (Rome).

31 *CIL* IV, 3775 and 3884.

32 *CIL* III, 633, I and II.

33 *L. Lat.* 8, 62.

34 *Ep.* III, 12, 5, Mohr.

35 *NH* XXXV, 128

36 A. M. Tamassia, *ArchClass* XIII (1961), pp. 124–131; G. Roux, *REA* LXIII (1961), pp. 5–14—both with bibliography.

37 Marquardt, *op. cit.* (note 28), p. 624, note 4. See the verb χαράσσω in the shop sign from Palermo discussed above.

38 *Satyr.* 65, 5.

39 Blümner, *op. cit.* (note 28), pp. 6–7; A. Jacob, 'Lapidarius', 'Lapicida', in Daremberg-Saglio, *Dict. Ant.*; Hug, *RE*, s.v. 'Lapidarius' (1924); G. Samonati, 'Lapicida, Lapidecaesor', 'Lapicidina', 'Lapidarius', in De Ruggiero, *Diz. ep.*

40 *CIL* VI, 33908; 33909.

41 Marquardt, *op. cit.* (note 28), pp. 623–624 and especially p. 623, note 6; on the doubts about the meaning of *quadrata littera* in Petronius, *Satyr.* 29, 1, see J. S. and A. E. Gordon, *Contributions*, pp. 21–22.

42 *CIL* VI, 33902.

43 I. Calabi-Limentani, 'Marmorarius', in *Enc. dell' Arte ant.*, IV (1961), pp. 870–875, with a list of signatures of *marmorarii*, and discussion of a wide range of related problems.

44 *CIL* VI, 9556= *ILS* 7679.

45 See, e.g., the Cyprian ones recently published by I. Michaeli-dou-Nikolaou, in *BCH* LXXXIX (1965), pp. 122–123.

46 See, e.g., the collection by L. Cosmi Bracchi, 'Orologi solari di Aquileia', in *Aquileia nostra* XXXI (1960), coll. 49–70.

47 This same technique was used during the late Empire, and especially in Byzantine times, to produce inscriptions with relief letters; before this, the technique (ἔκτυποι or πρότυποι)

had been used almost exclusively to produce the clay stamps which were impressed on bricks, amphorae and lamps by means of metal punches, commonly to be seen in our museums (see, for example, the specimens in the Archaeological Museum at Arezzo). Sometimes they come in the shape of signet rings, less often in the shape of a long-handled punch, as in the superb specimen now in Lyon, in the Fourvière Archaeological Museum.

48   Letters of this type, complete with hooks for insertion in the marble and often still showing traces of lead, are to be seen in several museums; for their exceptional state of preservation and their wealth of instrumental details, let me note the specimens in the Archaeological Museum at Tarracina, those in the National Museum at Budapest, and the gilded ones in the Archaeological Museum at Stuttgart which came from the legionary camp at Schierenhof. Obviously the same technique was used for those texts into which a metal object was inserted, either as a symbol or as a votive object: thus, e.g., the strigils on some stelae from Laconia (see the drawings in K. M. T. Chrimes, *Ancient Sparta*, Manchester 1952).

49   See J. Lassus, in *Lybica* VII (1959), pp. 143–146; technically analogous considerations will apply to the craftsmen who produce the pattern for tapestries and carpets.

50   Leclercq, 'Lapicides' (cited note 28), coll. 1331–1332.

51   Calabi, *op. cit.* (note 43); also *ibid.* p. 874, fig. 1039.

52   *Op. cit.* (note 28), pp. 217–226. See also *Mostra Aug. della Romanità, Cat.*, 4th ed., Roma 1938, pp. 648–650.

53   E. Espérandieu, *Recueil gén. des bas-reliefs de la Gaule rom.* II, Paris 1908, pp. 155–156, note 1111.

54   Blümner, *loc. cit.* (note 52), *a.*

55   Jacob, *op. cit.* (note 39), fig. 4342.

56   See *CIL* XIII, 8352, from Cologne.

57   Leclercq, *op. cit.* (note 28), coll. 1335–1337.

58   Calabi, *op. cit.* (note 43).

59   *Ibid.*; L. Friedländer, *Darstellungen aus der Sittengesch. Roms* II⁹, Leipzig 1920, pp. 361–365.

60   See the very rich collection by L. Bruzza, *Iscrizioni di marmi*

grezzi, in *Annali dell' Instituto di Corr. Arch.* XLII (1870), pp. 106–204; and J. Svennung, 'Numerierung von Fabrikaten u. anderen Gegenständen im römischen Altertum', *Arctos*, n.s., II (1958), pp. 164–186.

61 Perhaps this explains a set of numerals peculiar to some funerary stones from Padua; see F. Sartori, 'Una particolarità epigrafica di Patavium', *Mem. Acc. Patav.* LXXV (1962–1963), pp. 61–73.

62 *CIL* V, 8074.

63 *CIL* XIII, 5153.

64 *CIL* XI, 828.

65 Hübner, *op. cit.* (note 5), pp. 24–25; A. Moretti and J. B. Ward Perkins, s.v. 'Marmo', in *Enc. dell' Arte ant.* IV (1961), pp. 860–870.

66 *Fonti per la storia greca e romana del Salento*, Bologna 1962, pp. 59–65 and *passim*.

67 A. E. Gordon, *Epigraphica. On Marble as a Criterion for Dating Republican Latin Inscriptions. Univ. of California Publ. in Class. Arch.* I, 5, 1936, pp. 159–168.

68 Examples are innumerable; for an interesting case from Aquileia, see L. Bertacchi, *BA* 1964, p. 264, fig. 19.

69 Leclercq, *op. cit.* (note 6), col. 722, note 17. Cf. also the graffito inscription incised on a clay pyxis in the British Museum, which reads *Iucundi*; the last three letters had been written so carelessly that they were repeated in a second line.

70 S. Mariner Bigorra, 'Il problema degli epitafi ripetuti e le sue derivazioni', in *Atti terzo Congr.* (cited note 3), pp. 207–211.

71 Blümner, *op. cit.* (note 28), II, Leipzig 1879, pp. 200–210.

72 To mention one example, the stele of Pettia Ge from Regium Lepidi, where several instruments are represented (*CIL* XI, 951: our fig. 2).

73 On this subject, the essential bibliography will be found in B. Gabričević, *Arheološki Radovi i Rasprave* I (1959), pp. 299–310; S. Panciera, *Latomus* XIX (1960), pp. 701–707, with (p. 701, note 1) all the preceding bibliography, and *RAC* XXXV (1959), pp. 81–86; J. Rougé, *Latomus* XVIII (1959), pp. 649–653; E. Thévenot, *RAE* X (1959), pp. 142–148; F. de

Visscher, *BAB*, s. 5, XLIX (1963), pp. 309–318; and id., *Le Droit des Tombeaux romains*, Milano 1963, pp. 277–294; S. Ferri, *RAL*, s. 8, XVIII (1963), pp. 174–178. Note the expression *ab ascia fecit monimentum* in an inscription from Rome now in the Archaeological Museum at L'Aquila (*CIL* VI, 8931), which quite possibly indicates that the entire monument, right from the initial cutting of the stone, was made out of new (hence uncontaminated) material, and therefore ritually quite proper for use in the funerary *devotio*.

74   Blümner, *op. cit.* (note 28) II, pp. 213–216, and fig. 41 on p. 215; Hübner, *op. cit.* (note 5), pp. 30–31; J. de Foville, 'Scalptura', in Daremberg-Saglio, *Dict. Ant.*; Leclercq, 'Lapicides' (cited note 28), coll. 1329–1330, figs. 6773–6779, and especially fig. 6776.

75   See J. S. and A. E. Gordon, *Contributions*, p. 69, fig. 1.

76   *Contributions, passim.*

77   Blümner, *op. cit.* (note 28) II, pp. 196–199; Hübner, *loc. cit.* (note 74); G. Lafaye, 'Malleus', in Daremberg-Saglio, *Dict. Ant.*; Leclercq, *loc. cit.* (note 74).

78   Thylander, *op. cit.* (note 6), pp. 48–49; J. S. and A. E. Gordon, *Contributions*, pp. 183–185 and 216.

79   *CIL* VI, 32932.

80   Susini, *RAL*, s. 8, X (1955), pp. 240–242.

81   The partial use of movable letters may explain, e.g., how the sign Ɔ (=mulier) in an inscription from Benevento (*CIL* XI, 1875) was produced by cutting exactly the lower part of an S of a much larger module: perhaps the draft suggested this procedure. On the 'construction' of the letters in monumental writing and on the epigraphical examples useful for the study of this, see the very interesting contribution of G. Mardersteig, 'Leon Battista Alberti e la rinascita del carattere lapidario romano nel Quattrocento', in *IMU* II (1959), pp. 285–307.

82   The definition of 'module' is found in J. S. and A. E. Gordon *Contributions*, p. 89. A test study of a fairly large sample of Roman inscriptions originating from several workshops in Italy and in the European provinces does not support the conclusion that the production of the monuments, the squaring

of the epigraphic surfaces and the module of the letters were reckoned according to multiples of Roman units of measurement.

83 G. Cencetti, in *Archivio paleografico italiano*, n.s. II–III (1956–1957), p. 188. It is also useful to recall Cencetti's warning (*ibid.*, p. 184) on the importance of learning to distinguish the genuinely archaic inscription (i.e. the inscription which originates in the graffito) from the slovenly work which is the inevitable consequence of incompetence and clumsiness: the clearest example of this is the case, still frequent even now, of the reversed S.

84 See for example Hübner, *op. cit.*, pp. 31–32; A. Rehm, 'Die Inschriften', in *Handbuch der Archäologie* I, München 1939, pp. 182–238, and especially pp. 216–226.

85 A. Degrassi, *RFIC* LXXXVII (1959), p. 211.

86 M. Bollini, 'Massimino il Trace e il figlio in una iscrizione di Claterna', *Studi Romagnoli* XIV (1963), pp. 305–318.

87 'Inscriptiones', in Daremberg-Saglio, *Dict. Ant.*, pp. 532–533 and fig. 4068. The examples mentioned by Cagnat show obvious traces of *ordinatio* done with either a hard-pointed instrument or varnish, in that portion of the stone where the carving was not completed (cited there: *CIL* V, 6421; VIII, 9395; X, 30; 811 and 812).

88 Mallon, *Paléographie romaine* (cited note 2 and text), p. 58, with examples from Rome, Mérida and the province of Baetica; also *Libyca* III (1955), pp. 155–162: this article deals with an inscription in which the work of carving was interrupted because of a flaw in the stone (a fairly common occurrence in antiquity, which allows us to determine what was the state of preservation of the surface at the moment of production), and in which the rest of the text has been incised, graffito style, by the *ordinator*. Analogous to this is the case of an inscription from Dura Europos (*L'Année Epigr.* 1948, no. 124) also mentioned by Mallon. On the genesis and causes of errors in Etruscan inscriptions, with remarks on method, see A. J. Pfiffig, in *SE* XXXII (1964), pp. 183–205.

89 See above, note 51.

90   Cat. No. 127.

91   *Mostra Aug. della Romanità, Cat.*, 4th ed., Roma 1938, I, p. 649, no. 12 *a*.

92   See above, note 88.

93   Hübner, *op. cit.*, p. 31.

94   Ferrua, *loc. cit.* (note 19).

95   As we shall see, this runs counter to Mallon's opinion, since, according to him, an error is all the more useful in reconstructing the draft if it occurs in a common expression.

96   *MH* (cited note 1).

97   *Loc. cit.* (note 19).

98   *Sat.* I, 65–66.

99   I would explain thus, for instance, what appears in an inscription on a small urn in the *Cabinet des Médailles*, Cat., No. 4831, which reads: *D(is) M(anibus) | Sex(ti) Afrani | Augazontis | Sex(tus) Afranius | Epagathus | filio piissimo | fecit et.* Since after the last line there is still room for four more, I believe that the final *et* can be perfectly well explained—or at least, explained more easily than on any other view—if we assume that the engraver was in the habit of writing a certain formula, such as *fecit et sibi*, which was not in fact in the draft he received on this occasion.

100   *Dis | Manib(us) | Cn(aei) | Pomponi | Epaphroditi | Cissiani, | Aug(ustalis). | F(ilii) l(ugentes)* [or *(et) l(iberti)*] *p(osuerunt)* (*NSA* 1886, p. 100; F L P is on the stone).

101   This is particularly so in the case of the consular dates placed on the sides of honorary monuments.

102   *CIL* XI, 6831.

103   This phenomenon occurs above all in the second half of the second century after Christ, before the border produced by a mere trench (what we may call the 'border trench') came into use. That practice apparently originated from—or at least imitated—a technique prevalent in Celtic sculpture, and it may easily be yet another among the numerous elements borrowed, in the later Empire, by Gallo-Roman culture from the neighbouring regions.

104   As, for example, in the stele of T. Truppicus, from the Po

Delta, now in the Archaeological Museum at Cesena (Susini, *Atti e Memorie della Deputazione di Storia patria per le Province di Romagna*, n.s. V (1953–1954, publ. 1957), pp. 73–103).

105 As an example, see an inscription from Pannonia (A. Schober, *JÖAI* XVIII (1914), Beibl. p. 241, note 15, fig. 203).

106 For an instance of this last, much less common, see the stele of the Albinii (*CIL* XI, 6397) from Pesaro.

107 See, for example, the stele of T. Flavennius Probus (*CIL* XI, 6122) from Forum Sempronii.

108 Susini, *Imola nell'antichità*, Roma 1958, p. 191.

109 See the inscriptions from Rudiae in *Fonti* (cited note 66), nos. 48 and 50.

110 *Ibid.*, no. 63.

111 This, of course, does not apply to the *ordinatio* of mosaic inscriptions, which is still to be seen in the underlying layer, and which included the guidelines, the drawing of the letters and the design of the whole pattern at the same time.

112 See above, note 3.

113 See *Scriptorium* (cited note 3), p. 189, note 23, for an inscription from Timgad.

114 See above, note 70.

115 'Philologie et inscriptions', *REA* LXII (1960), pp. 362–382.

116 *CIL* III, 5528.

117 *CIL* VI, 25498.

118 *Op. cit.*, pp. 41–43.

119 Of course, the error too, in its psychological genesis, is a cultural fact, and sometimes a previous palaeographical misunderstanding can be surmised at the back of it, but all this is irretrievably lost in the past and cannot help us in arriving at a description of the writing as it appeared in the original draft.

120 With regard to this, some doubts seem to be implied in Degrassi's remarks cited note 85.

121 *Inscr. It.* X, 1, 689.

122 Leclercq, *op. cit.* (note 6), coll. 721–724. Obviously, the more common errors, and the least likely to impinge upon the attention of the reader, occurred in letters of less frequent use,

such as Z, often transcribed as S (a modern phenomenon as well: see above, note 83; as a curiosity see also the inscription on the entrance gate of an estate in the Lessini Mountains, which reads: DEROCKETO instead of DEROCHETO: *Le Vie d'Italia*, 1962, 2, p. 190); and in groups of letters destined to reproduce complex sounds (in modern times also; thus in Monfalcone, on the lintel of a house-door, we find *1862 | Padron | Antonio | Travisan | filgio* [sic, for *figlio*] | *di | Michaele*). Probably the Romans did not worry excessively about 'clean', neat texts—texts, that is, unspoiled by too many corrections; such, at least, is my impression. I am inclined to think that, in general, they were content to produce a fairly intelligible correction, as is the case in an inscription from Ostia (H. Bloch, *Scavi di Ostia*, III, 1, Roma 1955, p. 209), where the ITERVM has been changed to TERTIO by writing the syllable TIO of the latter over the RVM of the former, without removing the initial I.

123   *AJP* LXXXI (1960), p. 193.

124   I once more beg the indulgence of those specialists in Latin epigraphy who may find these constant references to inscribed monuments of later ages and of today inappropriate. I should like to point out, however, that few phenomena are as accurate a measure of the temperature of the political moment as the erasure of inscriptions and symbols. At times they are our only remaining evidence; thus, during the Fascist regime, the reminders of Mazzini and Garibaldi which smacked in any way of socialism or anti-clericalism were relegated to the same attics which today store the inscriptions recalling the 'Sanctions' over Ethiopia. It would be interesting to know what was once engraved under the present inscription for the Italian soldiers who died in the campaigns of 1860, to be seen at Spoleto in Piazza Campello: *Il XVII settembre MDCCCLX | una mano di soldati | italiani | condotti dal valoroso Brignone | espugnando la rocca | ne sgombrava i mercenari della tirannide | e rendeva a Spoleto la libertà |* etc. This last line was inserted in place of an earlier text by substituting a new block with different lettering at a later date. Let me end this extremely

brief survey of modern epigraphy by recalling good King Umberto I, whose name was erased from his Aosta monument and changed to 'Humbert Ier'. Truly, a history of our own 'speaking stones' would add considerably to our understanding of the various political and cultural environments of our past.

125 *CIL* VI, 16294.

126 Among the numerous useful instances, see the inscription in the Archaeological Museum at L'Aquila, *CIL* IX, 3440.

127 *CIL* XI, 600.

128 See for example the indication of the age of the deceased lady in the Assisi inscription now in the Archaeological Museum at Perugia, *CIL* XI, 5461: this indication was added on the upper edge of the frame, because the space between the lines was too narrow for any insertion and the text as it stands ends with the dedicator's name, making additions at the end impossible.

129 *Contributions* (cited p. 8), pp. 149–156.†

130 *CIL* VII, 189.

131 *BCH* LXXXIX (1965), p. 306.

132 *CIL* XI, 6283.

133 *CIL* X, 6330.

134 See Hübner, *op. cit.*, pp. 74–79.

135 This would also be my explanation for the blank spaces sometimes left on the stone by the stonecutter lacking certain data which he considers *de rigueur* in an inscription. Let me cite, as an instance, an inscription of Savaria, now in the Archaeological Museum at Szombathely (*AErt* 1961, pp. 249–252) where after the word *annor(um)* there is no numeral, but enough space is left to enter it later.

136 See the famous monument of Caesius Sabinus at Sarsina (*CIL* XI, 6489–6492).

137 *CIL* I², 1905 = *ILS* 5393a = *ILLRP* 619. Personal inspection enables me to correct *in agrum* (line 4 on the right side) to *in agro*; the former was, however, read in the other copy (now

† [Editor's note: But this is in fact not the meaning of 'centred' as used in that work.]

lost) of this inscription, *CIL* I² 1906=IX, 5076, where the 'crotchets' found on our stone are not indicated either. See *NSA* 1893, p. 352, with drawing.

138   *Libyca* III (1955), pp. 160–162, fig. 5.

139   'Sur les manuels professionels des graveurs d'inscriptions romaines', *RPh* XIII (1889), pp. 51–65; see Leclercq, *op. cit.* (note 28), coll. 1336–1343.

140   In addition to the contributions of Navascués (cited note 10), see, e.g., F. Diego Santos, *Epigrafía romana de Asturias*, Oviedo 1959; also J. Vives Gatell, 'Características regionales de los formularios epigráficos romanos', in *Actas del I Congreso Español de Estudios Clásicos*, Madrid 1958, pp. 485–492, particularly interesting for the distribution of *sigla* and formulae in the Roman West; C. Veny, *Corpus de las inscripciones Baleáricas hasta la dominación áraba*, Madrid 1963 (palaeographic index on pp. 280–282).

141   See, e.g., the article by W. Vollgraff in *AC* XIX (1950), pp. 165–167. The epigraphical environment in Mauretania is studied by P.-A. Février, *Mél. d'Arch. et d'Hist.* LXXVI (1964), pp. 105–172.

142   See *Fonti* (cited note 66).

143   'Le officine lapidarie romane di Ravenna', in *XII Corso di cultura sull'arte ravennate e bizantina*, Ravenna 1965, pp. 547–575.

144   'L'officina lapidaria di Urbino', in *Studi in onore di Luisa Banti*, Roma 1965, pp. 309–318.

145   'Épigraphie', in *L'Histoire et ses méthodes*, Paris 1961, pp. 453–495, and especially pp. 457–458.

146   See the survey of modern opinions in the work of Navascués cited in note 10; also the 'chronological criteria' proposed by the Gordons, in *Contributions*, pp. 208–217 (with the slight qualifications added by R. P. Oliver in *AJP* LXXXI (1960), pp. 189–197); finally, see A. Degrassi, *L'epigrafia latina in Italia nell'ultimo ventennio e i criteri del nuovo insegnamento*, Padova 1957, p. 10.

147   *Op. cit.* (note 6), p. 41.

148   *Atti terzo Congr.* (cited note 3), pp. 71–76.

149 'Chronologie des épitaphes romaines de Lyon', *REA* LXI (1959), pp. 320–352.

150 *Satyr.* 58, 7.

151 J. S. and A. E. Gordon, *Contributions*, pp. 73–74; see Bagnani, *op. cit.* (note 6), p. 20.

152 *Studi Romagnoli* XIII (1962, publ. 1964), pp. 175–190.

153 See the examples from Paestum and Palinurus: M. Guarducci, *NSA*, 1948, pp. 185–186, and *Apollo* II (1962, publ. 1964), pp. 3–7.

154 There are, nevertheless, instances of inscriptions on milestones of rectangular shape, especially in Pannonia, in Gallia Narbonensis and at Aquileia (G. Brusin, *AIV* CXIV (1955–1956), pp. 281–290); the development of the text from mere road direction to fully fledged honorary inscription was bound to promote frontality.

155 See the exceptionally good examples reproduced in *Le Vie d'Italia* 1958, pp. 57–64 (where a comparison is made between the 'epigraphic horizon' at night and during the day), pp. 881–883, and 1960, plate following p. 40.

156 Susini, *Officine epigrafiche e ceti sociali*, Urbania 1962, pp. 16–17. The same development can be surmised for the small cippi of conic or spheroidal shape from some Etruscan centres (especially Chiusi, Tuscania and Tarquinia), which were also used during the Roman period. The Etruscan workshops, however, also knew the stelae with rounded tops.

157 See the examples of the inscriptions of the *quaestores* from Bologna (*CIL* XI, 697 a and b; *ILS* 3629; Susini, *Il lapidario greco e romano di Bologna*, Bologna 1960, nos. 129 and 133, especially pp. 116-117).

158 G. A. Mansuelli, *PP* XXI (1966), p. 140.

159 A. Degrassi, in *Hommages à Albert Grenier*, Bruxelles 1962, pp. 510–512; see L. Pitimada, *NSA* 1953, pp. 343–344.

160 Susini, *ASAA* XLI–XLII (1963–1964, publ. 1965), pp. 212–213 and 219–224.

161 *Inscr. It.* XIII, 1, pp. 17–19.

162 'Archäologie und Epigraphik', *AA* 1948–1949, coll. 253–255.

163 *Op. cit.* (note 11).

164 'Monumento funerario', in *Enc. dell'Arte ant.* V (1963), pp. 170–202.

165 *Op. cit.* (note 84), pp. 213–215.

166 See, e.g., the inscription *CIL* V, 199, from the Catajo collection: R. Noll, *Griechische und lateinische Inschriften der Wiener Antikensammlung*, Wien 1962, no. 164.

167 See the cippus of Flavia Aphrodisia, found at Lyon in the Fourvière excavations. An analogous instance is offered by the monument from Populonia *CIL* XI, 7247.

168 *RH* (cited note 6), pp. 299–301; see J. Guey's remarks in 'Graffiti et inscriptions. Ce que le paléographe attend de l'archéologie', *Rhodania* XXXVI (1960), pp. 17–25.

169 *Op. cit.* (note 83), p. 199.

170 *RH* (cited n. 6), p. 312; cf. *ibid.*, pp. 302–303.

171 *PP* 1965, p. 39. See P. Romanelli, *REL* XLII (1964), pp. 99–111, on the mutually complementary value of all disciplines within the context of Classical studies.

172 *RH* (cited note 6), p. 312.

173 'Ce n'est pas un paradoxe que d'insister sur le profit, pour nos études épigraphiques, des journées de voyage où nous n'avons pas trouvé à copier une seule inscription : sur les hauts plateaux, dans les pâturages . . . à travers les immenses forêts de pins, solitaires et silencieuses, descendant au fond des vallons et remontant en lacets jusqu'au col où un nouveau paysage se découvre comme une carte; à la source, au bord du sentier, même si nous ne découvrons pas de dédicace aux Nymphes, les Nymphes sont là, présentes, au milieu des platanes et des lauriers-roses, et elles redonnent courage aux hommes et aux bêtes, comme elles ont fait pendant des siècles. . . .' (*Actes du IIe Congrès intern. d'Épigraphie*, Paris 1953, pp. 11–12).

174 'Épigraphie' (cited note 145), p. 453.

175 *Ibid.*, p. 454.

176 Innumerable examples might be presented to illustrate the nuclei of inscriptions characteristic of our own culture: I mention only a vivid one cited by C. D'Onofrio, in *Capitolium* XXXVI (1961), 4, p. 10; see also the useful remarks by G,

Ansaldo, in the magazine *Tempo*, XXIII, 40 (Oct. 7, 1961), p. 18.

177 See D. Villani, *Storia del manifesto pubblicitario*, Milano 1964, especially pp. 17–29.

178 *Paléographie romaine*, Madrid 1952, pp. 61–62.

179 Ἐπιγραφική, in Μεγ. Ἑλλην. Ἐγκυκλοπ. X (1954), pp. 879–880; cf. S. Charitonidis, Μνημειακὴ διαμόρφωσις τῶν ἐπιγραφῶν in Ἐπιστημικὴ Ἐπετερὶς τῆς φιλοσ. Σχολῆς, Thessaloniki, Suppl. 1 (1963).

180 For a different opinion, see G. A. Mansuelli, *SE*, Suppl. XXV (1959), p. 101.

INDEX OF INSCRIPTIONS DISCUSSED

References are to numbers of notes where the inscriptions are cited; the corresponding pages of text will readily be found. Occasional mention in the text only is shown by figures in italics, referring to page numbers. As a rule, only inscriptions for which an individual reference is given are recorded here, though a few references to small numbers of similar inscriptions published together are included for convenience. The few references to *ILS* given in the notes are not separately collected, but for each *CIL* inscription included in *ILS* the *ILS* reference has been added in parentheses.